Encountering Israel

Stephen J. Kramer

COMTEQ™
PUBLISHING
MARGATE, NEW JERSEY

Contact the author at: mskramer@jhu.edu

Published by:
    ComteQ Publishing
    A division of ComteQ Communications, LLC
    101 N. Washington Ave. • Suite 2B
    Margate, New Jersey 08402
    609-487-9000 • Fax 609-487-9099
    Email: publisher@ComteQpublishing.com
    Website: www.ComteQpublishing.com

ISBN 978-1-935232-23-0
Library of Congress Control Number: 2010930336

Cover design by Denis Lee
Book design by Stephen Kramer

Printed in the United States of America
10 9 8 7 6 5 4 3 2 1

CONTENTS

ENCOUNTERING ISRAEL – THE CENTER

ENCOUNTERING ISRAEL – THE NORTH

ENCOUNTERING ISRAEL – THE SOUTH

Preface

This book is intended for: armchair travelers (even if they live in Israel); travelers who have been to Israel; and those who intend to travel to Israel. My goal is to give readers a personal feeling for contemporary Israel, while not neglecting its tumultuous past. This book covers many of Israel's wonderful sites and locales, including some unusual, less touristic ones. After reading each vignette, you'll have a feeling for the geography, history and culture of the place, as if you've been there with me. Even better, you may decide to put down this book and tour Israel yourself!

An avid reader of mine, my mother, has commented that in nearly twenty years of touring Israel, I have yet to run out of interesting subjects. That's part of Israel excitement. There's an unbelievable number of attractions in a nation the size of the American state of New Jersey.

These articles have appeared in the Jewish Times of South Jersey, for which I have been the Israel correspondent since its inception.

Below is an explanation of some of the terms that are repeated throughout the book:

BCE: Before Common Era, corresponds to BC
CE: Common Era, corresponds to AD

yishuv: the Jewish community in Palestine before independence
kibbutz: originally a socialist-communist agricultural settlement
moshav: originally a cooperative agricultural community
aliyah: the act of immigrating to Israel; literally "going up"

IDF: Israel Defense Forces (army, navy, air force)

JNF: Jewish National Fund, known as KKL in Israel

oriental: adjective meaning Arab-style

Green Line: the 1949 Armistice Line (not a formal border) delineating the disputed area between Israelis and Palestinians, which was occupied by Jordan between 1948-1967

Holidays - Pesach/Passover, Shavuot / Shavuos or Weeks, Succot / Succos or Tabernacles

Safed: city in northern Israel; also spelled Tzvat or Zefat

Kinneret: large lake in northern Israel, same as Sea of Galilee

Dead Sea: extremely salty lake.at the lowest spot on earth

nahal: river or stream, sometimes dry
wadi: dry river bed

Western Wall: remnant of the retaining wall of the Temple Mount, called the Wailing Wall before its liberation in 1967

ESRA: English Speaking Resident Association, an Israeli charitable and social club in Israel

Zionism: national movement for the return of the Jewish people to their homeland; the resumption of Jewish sovereignty in Israel

I highly recommend "Jerusalem - a walk through time" by Yad Ben-Zvi (two volumes), which I've consulted frequently.

This book was greatly improved by my editors, Michal Kramer and Linda Glazer, and my proofreaders, Howard Epstein and Ros Harari. My wife Michal was of invaluable assistance.

Stephen J. Kramer, June, 2010

Encountering Israel – the Center

HIGHLIGHTS IN RED – JEZREEL AND ELAH VALLEYS

Starting in February, Israelis literally head for the hills. The national character includes a healthy dose of tramping through fields and valleys searching for as many varieties of wildflowers as possible. In the past few months we've been on three day trips to enjoy the fresh air and to see a myriad of colored flowers: red (the favorite), white, blue, violet, yellow, pink, purple and probably more. The ultimate experience is to see as many varieties as possible in one area. Below are highlights of those trips, ending with a very special ceremony of green turning to red.

On the spur of the moment, we headed north to the Jezreel Valley, the largest in Israel, which divides the Galilee and Samaria regions. In biblical times its largest settlements were Megiddo, Yizre'el and Bet Shean. Zionist newcomers started settling there in the 1920s and built many agricultural settlements. Today, Afula and Bet Shean are its primary towns.

We soon arrived at one of the loveliest JNF locations, Hazorea (Sowers) Forest. The JNF has planted millions of trees in Israel since before the War of Independence in 1948. In Hazorea Forest, the 3-dimensional quality of the landscape, with cypress trees in the foreground and the heavily forested Carmel range of mountains behind was very impressive. The flowers, of course, were profuse and beautiful. We walked in the same woods where Palmach soldiers secretly trained before the War of Independence. The Palmach was the precursor to the Israel Defense Forces. Another interesting aspect of this JNF hiking site is that a large portion of it is wheelchair accessible. We walked primarily in the furthermost areas where there were fewer families and enjoyed a great al fresco picnic before returning home. Total time for this quick trip to a different world was only about six hours.

Even closer was another hike in Tel Aviv's Hayarkon National Park, located about twenty minutes from our home in Alfe Menashe. This park covers the area from the Roman-era ruins of Antipatris to the spring at Rosh Ha'ayin, the source of the Yarkon River. The Yarkon meanders through the countryside for about twenty miles before cleaving Tel Aviv and emptying into the Mediterranean Sea. Rainwater from the mountains of Judea and Samaria is the source of the spring which pours 200 million cubic meters of water into the Yarkon annually, making it the second largest river - after the Jordan River - in Israel. Because of the diversion of most of its water to the national water carrier, the Yarkon River appears quite small. Unfortunately, most of the river is polluted beyond the confines of the park, but the pollution is slowly being reduced by environmental agencies.

Within the park, conservation and rehabilitation works have created a lovely public recreation spot with trails, wooden walkways, bike paths, and loads of picnic areas. An added attraction is Antipatris, where there are remnants of an impressive Ottoman fortress, built in 1571, the remains of an Egyptian Governor's palace (dating to 1200-1550 BCE), and the remains of the ancient Cardo (main street), of the Roman city of Antipatris. Herod the Great built Antipatris to honor his father, Antipater. Herod is most famous for building Masada, Caesarea, and his extensive renovations of the Second Temple in Jerusalem.

On another day, traveling towards Jerusalem, we hiked in the vicinity of Beit Shemesh. This was another occasion to see colorful flowers in profusion. The most interesting historical aspect of the hike was when we passed through the Elah Valley. We were at the site where David is thought to have chosen five smooth stones from a brook to put into his shepherd's bag. Shortly afterward David slew Goliath with his sling, which eventually led to David's reign as Israel's second king. At the end of the hike we had a delicious and interesting meal at a rustic farm which specializes in homemade goat cheeses. The food, consisting of cheese, salads, olives, stuffed fig leaves, wine, and tea was delicious, but the rainy weather didn't allow us to sit outdoors in the nearby flowering meadow, so we shivered in the partially enclosed shelter that served as a dining room. Nevertheless, it was an unforgettable experience.

The Elah Valley is on the way to the Etzion bloc of settlements, which are close to Jerusalem. We heard the story of a very determined group of hikers who preceded us long ago during the War of Independence. Thirty-eight fighters set out from the Mediterranean coastal area to assist the villagers who were battling Arab forces attacking the Etzion settlements. One warrior was badly injured on the way and had to turn back, helped by two others. The remaining thirty-five continued on towards their goal. Along the way, they saw an old shepherd tending his flock. Deciding that he was harmless, they ignored him and carried on. Evidently, the shepherd was able to communicate his sighting of the Jewish force and they were ambushed – none survived. The Arabs defeated the residents of Etzion and destroyed the village. After the Six Day War of 1967, the area was retaken and the villages were rebuilt. The road that we traveled on our lovely hike is named "The Way of the 35" in honor of the brave soldiers who were killed defending their land.

It's appropriate that I spoke of warriors, because the last event I will chronicle is not another hike, but the ceremony that we attended at Ammunition Hill in Jerusalem, marking the graduation from inductee to warrior for our son Shaul and his fellow paratroopers. The importance of this site dates back to the Six Day War of 1967, when Israeli paratroopers were ordered to capture Ammunition Hill and its fortified Jordanian Police Training School, which proved crucial to gaining access to the Old City. In four hours of battle thirty-six men lost their lives. But this day marked a happier occasion for all of us.

The ceremony was preceded by a two-day, fifty-five mile march for the recruits, with full equipment and carrying stretchers. This is the most arduous march of all the IDF (Israel Defense Forces) battalions. After the boys had time to rest a few hours, shower, and change uniforms, they proceeded to Ammunition Hill to rehearse for the ceremony. Family and friends arrived late in the afternoon to see hundreds of green-clad soldiers, some limping, some on crutches, but all looking elated and exhausted. Except for the officers, they all wore inductees' olive-drab berets. As the ceremony progressed, various soldiers, and then whole platoons, were congratulated by their officers and presented the coveted red beret of the Paratroop Brigade. The sea of green berets gradually became redder and redder. Eventually, all that we saw were red berets capping the heads of the young men.

As we walked away from the ceremony with Shaul (whose legs seemed to have turned to cement), we were proud that all these recruits had made it through their arduous basic training. Now begins the hard part: to be on guard and to fight to retain Israel's independence and our very existence as a nation. Since every paratrooper is a volunteer, they are very aware of their mission. Because of them and all the other soldiers and reservists that comprise the Israel Defense Forces, Israelis are able to roam the countryside enjoying the flowers. We can't forget, for even a moment, that without the IDF there would be no Jewish State.

TEL AVIV'S CHALLENGE TO ZIONISM

Paradoxically, the growth of Tel Aviv was a major challenge to the Zionism of Israel's founding fathers. This unexpected conclusion was proven to the audience at this year's first lecture of the English-Speaking Friends of Tel Aviv University. Dr. Haim Fireberg, a specialist in urban history in the Jewish History Department of TAU, spoke to us on the topic: Tel Aviv and the Zionist Vision of Eretz Yisrael.

The history of Tel Aviv began about a century ago - the official centennial date is 2009. Actually, it began before that, in the dreams of hundreds of pioneers who came to Israel in the late 19th century and who settled in the ancient port city of Jaffa. Chafing under the need to spread out from the crowded, mostly Arab city, in 1906 a group of pioneers formed a society called Ahuzat Bayit (homestead), to establish a new neighborhood based on scientific urban planning. In 1908, using funds borrowed from the Jewish National Fund, twelve acres of sand dunes northeast of Jaffa were purchased and divided into 60 plots.

On May 21, 1910, Ahuzat Bayit adopted Tel Aviv as the name for the new city, acting in conjunction with two other pioneering societies. The name means "Hill of Spring" and it was chosen because of its associations with rebirth and revitalization. In addition, it had been used by Nahum Sokolow as the title of his Hebrew translation of Theodor Herzl's novel "Altneuland". In that book, Herzl described a European-style garden suburb next to Jaffa, containing wide streets and boulevards. With high hopes, the Jewish pioneers began the building of such a city. Tel Aviv was expected to be inhabited only by Jews who spoke Hebrew. Its model was New York City. (Even today, Israelis like to think of Tel Aviv as a little New York.)

The pioneers' ambition to leave Jaffa and build a city on sand dunes sounds like Zionism at its best. This was not the case, however, for all Zionists. From its beginning, Zionism was a political movement of two main streams. The first was Social Zionism, a pastoral ideology which imagined a socialist, agrarian homeland for the Jews, built on Jewish labor. It was led by David Ben-Gurion and its adherents were mainly Russian socialists and communists. Revisionist Zionism, led by Ze'ev Jabotinsky, was a more nationalistic ideology and followed more closely the blueprint envisioned by Theodor Herzl.

David Ben-Gurion's faction became more prominent in the Yishuv to the detriment of the Revisionists. This being the case, the Social Zionists pushed for smaller, agrarian communities instead of large cities in the European mold. Obviously, the prospect of a large city - Tel Aviv - populated by small shopkeepers and tradesmen, was not what Ben-Gurion was promoting. Tel Aviv's growing size and importance was in opposition to the Zionist rural ethos, even though it was what Herzl had foreseen and written about.

The growth of the city was not without its problems. It couldn't be planned in the conventional sense because the ruling Ottoman Turks constrained Tel Aviv's growth during its first decade. However, within a decade the Turks were defeated in WWI and usurped by Britain. But the British were also intent on limiting the ambitions of the Jews throughout Palestine. Nevertheless, Tel Aviv's first mayor, Meir Dizengoff (a founding member of Ahuzat Bayit), was able to say in 1922 that Tel Aviv was "an ultra-modern city that is exclusively Jewish" and that it was the "most important Jewish experiment in 2,000 years".

Tel Aviv's rapid growth, especially during the 1930s with the influx of German refugees, was viewed with consternation by the Social Zionists, who were trying to create a "new Jew". Tel Aviv was bursting with bourgeois Jews who didn't know one end of a shovel from the other. Unfortunately for Ben-Gurion and his followers, the city dwellers could do very well without the produce of the Jewish agriculturists (there were plenty of Arab peasant farmers), but the country folk couldn't get on without the commerce that emanated from Tel Aviv. The only solution for the Social Zionists was to try to take control of the municipality. In the 1920s they went so far as to run Golda Meir for mayor of Tel Aviv. She lost.

In the period between the early 1920s and Israel's War of Independence in 1948, Tel Aviv grew to be something of a city-state. The Social Zionist leaders and the Histadrut (the huge, socialist trade union) watched glumly as the city tripled in size to 160,000 by the late-1930s, with a budget that eventually grew larger than that of the Jewish Agency, the Yishuv's largest institution. Nevertheless, Britain did prevent the city's leaders from enlarging the boundaries of the city. The result is that the cities of Bnei Berak, Ramat Gan, Givatayim and Petah Tikva are all contiguous to Tel Aviv but remain separate from it and each other. This is in contrast to New York City, which expanded to include Brooklyn, once America's third largest city, and three other adjacent areas. If it had been up to Tel Aviv's founders, the city would have become a metropolis stretching thirty miles along Israel's coast, as far north as Netanya.

Jaffa, once the largest Arab city in Palestine, today is part of the Tel Aviv municipality. As noted, Tel Aviv began as a small suburb of Jaffa. But by 1936, with the outbreak of the Arab riots, Mayor Dizengoff urged that the Jewish Agency's offices be opened in Tel Aviv. He also succeeded in establishing a separate port there. With these accomplishments, Tel Aviv had become totally independent of Jaffa and its port, segregating Jews in the new city from Arabs in the old town. The situation changed just a dozen years later, when during the War of Independence, Jewish fighters defeated the Arabs who were firing on them from Jaffa. The Jewish army conquered Jaffa in 1948 and the Tel Aviv municipality took effective control of all services there. In 1950, the reunification with Tel Aviv was formalized.

Dr. Fireberg summed up his introduction to the history of Israel's first Hebrew city by contrasting the visions of Ben-Gurion and Dizengoff. Ben-Gurion venerated the old 19th century European ideal of rural communities and medium-sized cities, with a large dash of socialism thrown in. Dizengoff shared Herzl's vision of a futuristic, thriving, and dynamic metropolitan society. As anyone who visits Israel can see, the visions of both men have been realized as Greater Tel Aviv has nearly three million people and is Israel's cultural capital. I think that contemporary Israel represents a fusion of Theodor Herzl's vision for "Altneuland" (Old New Land) with the pragmatic Zionism of the founding fathers.

THE YEMENITE QUARTER OF TEL AVIV

When I first traveled to Israel as a tourist, I had the impression that Tel Aviv was not an essential destination to visit during a short trip — not special or worth wasting valuable time on. Since moving to Israel, we have discovered quite the opposite — Tel Aviv is unequaled by any other Israeli city for its liveliness and trendiness, as well as its (modern) history as a spin-off of ancient Jaffa. In addition, UNESCO has designated Tel Aviv a World Heritage Site as "The White City", the world's largest assemblage of Bauhaus architecture – some 4,000 buildings in one sq. mile.

My wife and I recently explored the Yemenite Quarter, built on sand dunes overlooking the Mediterranean Sea. In the late 19th and early 20th centuries, Jaffa - then predominantly Arab - was also home to many Jews who had made aliyah (immigrated), including a significant number of Yemenite Jews. Since the cemetery which served Jaffa's Jewish population was miles away across hot sands, one enterprising Yemenite built a shack supplying refreshments for the hot, tired mourners on their way there. Within a few years, that one shack had become a small village which, as the city of Tel Aviv rose from the sand dunes, became the Yemenite Quarter.

Yemen is located at the southern tip of the Arabian Peninsula on the Gulf of Aden, by the mouth of the Red Sea. Most historians date Jewish settlement in Yemen from the time of the destruction of the First Temple in 586 BCE, or more likely from the dispersion of most Jews from the Land of Israel by the Romans in 70 CE, concurrent with the destruction of the Second Temple. The Yemenite Jews left their domicile of a few thousand years for two reasons. The first was the age-old desire to return to Zion (Jerusalem), the center of Jewish life. The second was to flee the Muslims, who resented the Jews ever since Mohammed failed to convert the plentiful Jews of the Arabian Peninsula, a resentment enflamed by the rebirth of Israel.

Mohammed stated that man's natural religion was Islam, and that he was its last and greatest prophet (after Moses and Jesus). In Yemen, if someone who had been raised as a non-believer (Jew or Christian) became an orphan or was separated from his family, he was to be returned to his "true" faith, Islam. Consequently, young Jewish children were at risk of being kidnapped and forcibly converted. Numerous young, Jewish boys fled Yemen by water to nearby Ethiopia, then north by foot to Egypt, and eventually to the Land of Israel. Entire families also came, mostly in the great migration known to Westerners as Operation Flying Carpet, or as the Yemenites called it, the Wings of Eagles. To the relatively backward Yemenites, the giant aircraft which ferried them to the State of Israel after its re-founding in 1948 resembled the giant eagles that had been prophesied in the Torah to speed their return to Zion (Exodus 19:4).

The Yemenite Quarter today is in the process of gentrification. It is known especially for the covered Carmel Market it borders and the many restaurants which are busy night and day serving typical Yemenite oriental fare. The Yemenites were predominantly devout Jews with large families. Now their descendants live throughout Israel and the Quarter is also home to numerous other nationalities. Our guide told us many stories about colorful individuals, including one old, white-bearded patriarch who smiled pleasantly at us from his yard while we listened to great tales about him in English, a language which he doesn't know. A child of one of the first settlers in the Quarter, he has scores of grandchildren and great-grandchildren. Who knows what will become of this nonagenarian's valuable property when he is unable to climb the flight of stairs to his tiny synagogue next door? It's there that he reads (or perhaps has memorized) the entire service in Hebrew and Aramaic. Homes like his, which are eventually left to multiple descendants, are typical of many of the dilapidated properties in the Quarter.

We've eaten in several restaurants in the Yemenite Quarter, some fancy and some holes-in-the-wall, but all with excellent food. Because the Quarter is next to the trendy Neve Tzedek which boasts great restaurants and cafés, some notable small museums, and the Suzanne Dellal Center for Dance and Theater, its quaint alleys and tiny homes are being transformed into a very expensive neighborhood. There's even a huge condominium tower looming above the area, much to the chagrin of the residents. However, the municipality's plans to upgrade the large Carmel Market are a sign that the Yemenite Quarter's charm as both a neighborhood and tourist attraction will probably ensure its survival.

FULL MOON RISING – THE ALEXANDER RIVER

We recently enjoyed a very special evening excursion. This was one of the nighttime hikes which Israelis delight in when the moon is at its fullest. Years ago, shortly after we had moved to Israel, we did one of these hikes in the Negev Desert, with its awesome landscape and incredible night sky. Our most recent hike, however, was much closer to home.

In the early evening, after work, we joined a busload of friends and acquaintances, all affiliated with ESRA, a terrific organization of English-speaking Israelis who do great charitable deeds and have fun too. (www.esra.org.il) We joined the rush-hour traffic for about an hour to arrive at our starting point, just north of Netanya. We planned to walk just 3.5 miles along the Alexander River and to end up at the beach for a late supper and entertainment. The provenance of the river's name is obscure, but it is probably named after (Jewish) King Alexander Yannai, or perhaps Alexander the Great. Since the river intersected the ancient coastal road from Alexandria to Damascus, Alexander's troops would have crossed it.

At first, before the moon rose, we relied on our flashlights to enhance our night vision. But it wasn't too long before our first sight of the gorgeous, huge, harvest moon rising above the horizon. If you've seen such a moon, you'll remember that it looks almost like a pale sun. I've seen only a few that equaled the beauty of this one. While the Alexander River is no rushing torrent, the trail alongside of it is landscaped and maintained beautifully by the JNF/KKL (Jewish National Fund). It was only after moonrise that we were able to enjoy the trail fully. As the evening progressed, the sky got brighter and brighter as the moon reached its zenith. A few times we stopped by the banks or on a convenient bridge to look for the famous soft shell turtles, which are found only here and up north in Akko. Unfortunately, they must have been sleeping, because not one responded to the bread and apple cores that we threw into the water.

Further along, we came across a beautiful outdoor party venue. In America, especially in urban areas, there are some wedding halls, but in Israel there are many, each nicer than the next. Especially interesting are those like the one on the Alexander's bank, in a natural setting. These "halls" are strictly for warm weather events, since all the festivities are outside. Usually there is no rainfall in Israel from May until September, which allows the scheduling of many parties. Since a wedding was being conducted just when we arrived at the party area, we had to take a quick detour around the parking lot to avoid interfering with the ceremony. It was lovely, though, to regain the trail in sight of the huppa (wedding canopy), and hear the rabbi chanting the wedding blessings as we walked silently by. Just a bit further on, we positioned ourselves in the exact spot to see the reflection on the water of the wedding lights, framed by a bridge, with the gorgeous moonlight shining down. Awesome!

We traveled on until we came to a beautiful mansion, abandoned long ago. Our guide related this story: A wealthy Arab family lived there and had the tax-collecting commission from the Ottoman Turks for river commerce, which consisted mainly of watermelons transported on rafts. The son of the family had often seen the beautiful daughter of a poor Beduin clan as she did the weekly laundry on the other side of the river. One thing led to another and they fell in love. The rich father would not hear of his son consorting with a poor nomad and forbade him to see her. But the couple loved each other so much that an angel came to them and told them to build a bridge of straw so that they could meet in the center. The angel cautioned them to let their love guide them, for the bridge was fragile and needed their unwavering faith to support their weight. The couple built the bridge from either bank and met in the middle. All was well until they became fainthearted and the flimsy structure collapsed, drowning them both. The wealthy tax collector was so distraught that he moved his family out of the house and away from the river, leaving only the abandoned structure for us to enjoy.

We continued along the river path until we heard the traffic on the coastal highway and could feel the humid, warmer air from the sea. Our bus met us there and we continued on to the beach, where we laid out our simple meal of salads, cold cuts, rolls and drinks. After eating, we were entertained by several of the group who had brought along poems to read and songs to sing. By the time we left after midnight, we all were satiated from the food and drink and tired from the walk. An evening hike can be more difficult than one by day because one's footing is not so assured. But this route had been so enjoyable that we planned to return with our friends during daylight to do it again.

THE SANCTITY OF JERUSALEM

Professor Dan Bahat is a dashing figure - erect carriage, bald dome, and huge mustache. He is known as "Israel's Indiana Jones" in Toronto, where he is professor of Jewish Studies in Jerusalem at St. Michael's College, University of Toronto. We attended one of his lectures at the Tel Aviv University, during one of his frequent trips to his native Israel. With a PhD from Hebrew University, where he formerly taught, and his experience as District Archeologist of Jerusalem, Bahat was well-qualified to address the crowd on the religious history of Jerusalem.

The professor began his engaging lecture by stating simply that the source of sanctity of Jerusalem is unequivocally Mt. Moriah, whose name means Foundation Stone. Mt. Moriah is the place where Abraham took his son Isaac when God called on him for a sacrifice, the place where the First and Second Temples were built, the place where the child Jesus is said to have chastised the money-lenders, and the current site of the Dome of the Rock, El Aksa mosque and the Western Wall. But the city of Jerusalem wasn't founded by the ancient Israelites - it was the Jebusites, a Caananite tribe, who first settled in the area. The name Jerusalem comes from "Jeru", signifying the Jebusites, and "Shalem", who was a Caananite deity, the god of darkness or night. King David captured the city from the Jebusites in about 1,000 BCE. The site of the even-then renowned Mt. Moriah would serve David as his "neutral" capital, as he successfully combined the southern kingdom, whose capital was Hebron, with the newly-won northern kingdom, whose capital was Shechem (today the Palestinian city of Nablus).

King David first settled at the foot of Mt. Moriah in the area known to us as David's City. (Today David's City, known as Silwan by its Arab inhabitants, has been repopulated by Jews.) David created a city, a dynasty, a nation, and a sanctuary for the Ark of the Covenant in Jerusalem. While David chose the location of the First Temple, planned its design, and procured the precious construction materials from King Hiram of Lebanon, David's son, King Solomon, built the Temple on the summit of Mt. Moriah, overlooking David's City. Professor Bahat emphasized King David's messianic qualities: he was born in Bethlehem, he was known as a "son of God", and he died in Jerusalem.

Around 700 BCE, the era when the kingdom of Babylonia was dominant in the region, the Jews celebrated Passover and the two other pilgrimage festivals in Jerusalem, trekking from all over the kingdom to offer sacrifices at the Temple. By this time, the Jews had internalized the city of Jerusalem as their center, surrounding Mt. Moriah, which they thought of as the "navel" of the world.

When King Nebuchadnezzar of Babylonia conquered Jerusalem in 586 BCE and carried off most of its inhabitants to Babylon, Jerusalem's status was immortalized by Psalm 137, which is famous for expressing the sentiments: "By the rivers of Babylon, there we sat down, yea, we wept, when we remembered Zion (Jerusalem).If I forget you, O Jerusalem, may my right hand lose its skill. May my tongue cling to the roof of my mouth if I do not remember you, if I do not consider Jerusalem my highest joy."

Professor Bahat emphasized that Jerusalem became sanctified in a long process lasting about 500 years, from the construction of the First Temple in Solomon's reign until the Second Temple was built following the return to Jerusalem of a remnant of the Jews from exile in Babylon. This happened about fifty years after the destruction of the First Temple in 586 BCE. (The Second Temple was later famously and gloriously enlarged by King Herod.)

In the Second Temple period, politics and religion mixed together in Jerusalem. Many different religious groups began to reside there, especially from the 1st-century BCE until the 2nd century CE. The Christians, one of the sects which resided in Jerusalem, first thought of themselves as Jews and they associated with Jews. They congregated in the eastern portico of the Temple before its destruction by the Romans in 70 CE. But as time went on, the Christians separated themselves from the Jews and gained pagan converts.

Hadrian, the Roman emperor from 117-138 CE, fought the second Roman war against the Jews and attempted to root out Judaism, which he considered a source of rebellion. It was Hadrian who blotted out the name Judea and renamed it Syria Palaestina (Palestine). It was also Hadrian who decided to rebuild the destroyed Jerusalem, renaming it Aelia Capitolina. He built a huge Temple of Jupiter on the Second Temple site. Jews were forbidden to enter the pagan city and were not even allowed to be in sight of the city. Nevertheless, scattered communities of Jews managed to remain, as they had during the period of Babylonian captivity.

It was Helena, mother of the (Christian) Roman Emperor Constantine (272-337 CE) who first put the stamp of Christianity on Jerusalem. She came to Palestine in her later years and had two churches erected for the worship of God: one in nearby Bethlehem near the Grotto of the Nativity, the other on the Mount of Olives in

Jerusalem. During her sojourn in Jerusalem, Helena tried to locate the exact site of Jesus' crucifixion, burial, and resurrection, which eventually resulted in Constantine building Christianity's holiest site, the Church of the Holy Sepulcher. By the 5th century CE, Jerusalem had become sacred for Christians, who came to view the purported tomb of Jesus and the tombs of the saints.

In the year 638, Caliph Omar conquered the city and surveyed the Temple Mount, which was covered in garbage by the Christians, who believed that this would bring them good luck. Omar gave certain rights to the city's Christian inhabitants but continued the ban on Jews living there. He built a modest mosque on the southern part of the Temple Mount where El-Aksa Mosque now stands, positioned so that during prayers worshipers faced east towards Mecca. Significantly, Omar ignored the advice of his adviser, the Jewish convert Kha ab al-Akhbar, who had recommended building a mosque to the north of the Foundation Stone (the summit of Mt. Moriah), so that the faithful would face both the sacred Jewish site and Mecca during prayers. Omar recognized Mecca as the unique focus of Islam, therefore a view of the Foundation Stone was superfluous during prayers.

The Muslims adopted Jerusalem, which they call Al Kuds (taken from the Hebrew for "holy city"), as their third holiest place, behind Mecca and Medina. Mohammed had first signified Jerusalem as the direction to which his followers should pray in an attempt to convince the Jews to convert. When that failed, Muhammad reverted to praying towards Mecca, which had been the pre-Islamic, pagan tradition of the Arabs. In 691, after Muhammad's death, the Damascus-based Umayyad dynasty fought off rival claims from Mecca and Medina (the Hejaz) for leadership of the faith. They attempted to glorify the status of Damascus as well as Jerusalem. In Jerusalem they built the Dome of the Rock shrine on top of the Foundation Stone, the site of the First and Second Temples.

The Umayyads then interpreted a passage of the Koran to identify the Dome of the Rock as the site of the "furthest mosque" to which Muhammad rode his horse on his "night journey". Though the proof that the Dome of the Rock is the "furthest mosque" is sketchy at best, nevertheless the Muslims, especially after the Six Day War of 1967, have made the claim of Jerusalem as their third holiest site into a call to war against the Jews.

Professor Bahat summarized his feelings about the undisputed primacy of the Jewish sanctity of Jerusalem by stating that the United Nations has never understood the facts regarding Jerusalem. For Bahat, the Muslims venerate solely the Temple Mount and the Christians venerate distinct holy sites which are strictly delineated, ignoring the Temple Mount. Only the Jews hold the entire city of Jerusalem holy and have done so for at least 2,500 years.

JERUSALEM WEEKEND

We started our weekend on Thursday night in front of the Kotel (Western Wall). Our older son Moshe was present with all the members of his induction group for the "swearing in" ceremony of the Paratroopers. It was grand seeing all the young men lined up in their units, all spit and polish, while the senior officers spoke about the importance of the role of the Paratroopers. Then, a Tanach (Hebrew Bible) was slipped under each soldier's shirt, near the heart, to symbolize love of Israel and Judaism. (The proportion of Paratroopers who are Orthodox is impressive). The climax of the ceremony was when all the inductees shouted out "I swear", in response to the declaration that they would honor their country and protect it by their military prowess. But more significant to me was the aftermath of the swearing in, seeing all the young men greeting their families and friends with such obvious feeling, and congratulating each other with such obvious warmth. It is clear that basic training imbues love of country and comradeship with their fellow soldiers in the young men. Michal and I couldn't ignore the fact that soon their lives may depend on the men with whom they are training.

After driving home late, we returned early the next morning to meet our hiking group at the Jaffa Gate in Jerusalem. Yossi, our guide on a recent tour in the Galilee, led us again. We had returned to the Kotel, but now we were embarking on the Jerusalem Tunnel tour, which Michal and I have tried to schedule without success a few times previously. This time we made it! The tour takes you under the existing street level of the plaza, parallel to the Western Wall, in areas dating back to the Hasmonean period (167-63 BCE). All of us were overwhelmed to be in the environs of the

First Temple. At one point we reached the spot closest to the original site of the Holy of Holies, which was at the center of both the First and Second Temples. Eventually we found ourselves in close quarters, a very narrow tunnel, which at one time was a watercourse for ancient Jerusalem. At the end of the tunnel Yossi had us retrace our steps backwards to the entrance, instead of exiting into the Arab Quarter, which was the scene of a violent riot when the Jerusalem Tunnel exit there was first opened to tourists.

We spent time walking through the Jewish Quarter, including a rooftop vista that gave us a different perspective of the Old City. We looked over a large portion of the Old City and beyond towards Mount Scopus. Following lunch, we left that section of the city and drove to the campus of the Mormon Jerusalem Center, next to the Hebrew University, where Christian students from abroad (mostly Mormon) can spend a semester. The buildings are magnificent, as are the gardens. Michal and I had not been here before, either. We were enchanted by the architecture and the incredible view towards the Old City. There were few students on campus at the time, however, because of a US government's travel advisory.

Completing our tour around the city, we drove to the Sherover and Hess Promenades in Talpiot, beautiful walkways with gardens, where our view was across town to the Old City and beyond it to the Mormon Center. Although Jerusalem is writ large in the imagination of the world for its religious importance and its beauty, its actual physical size is small enough to allow a trip like ours, which displayed its main points from a circular perspective in less than a day.

Tired, with eyes smarting from the glare of the sun on the omnipresent, pink Jerusalem stone, we retreated for the evening to Ein Karem, a lovely wooded village tucked away on the outskirts of Jerusalem. Today Ein Karem is a trendy suburban enclave with homes adjacent to many Christian churches and monasteries, which date back centuries. We stayed at the Notre Dame de Sion monastery, where we enjoyed a great dinner and clean rooms, plus an ample breakfast. After enjoying the monastery gardens, we drove downtown to the beginning of Jaffa Road, which we walked nearly to its end.

Among the highlights of the Jaffa Road tour were the stories Yossi told us about buildings along the street. We saw the grave of Dr. Moshe Wallach, the founder of Shaare Zedek, Jerusalem's first Jewish hospital. He forced patients to stand at prayer times, regardless of their ailments. Wallach was also responsible for the death of a young patient whom he would not allow to be admitted until after the end of Shabbat. Despite his failings, he is still revered by many for his many accomplishments. We passed through the outdoor Mahaneh Yehuda Market, deserted on Shabbat, which is thronged by shoppers during the week. We saw one of the oldest yeshivas (institutions for Torah study) in the city, where we learned about the drastic disciplinary measures that the students were subjected to. We passed the "dead groom's house", a magnificent mansion which the groom's parents built for him and his intended. The groom died the day before his wedding, but the marriage was performed anyway — with the groom dressed in his wedding suit — at the insistence of the parents.

Eventually we reached the end of Jaffa Road, regrouped and drove a short distance to Talbiyeh, a lovely neighborhood where the President's House is located. We walked through the neighborhood, admiring the beautiful houses, including that of Gita Sherover, who funded the promenade we visited the previous day. Across the street from her house is the Jerusalem Theater, and down the street is the former Leper Hospital, vacant, but sitting on very valuable real estate. The group then moved on to the "Jerusalem (Time Travel) Elevator", but since Michal and I had seen that attraction once before, we left the group, exhausted but buoyed by our sightseeing.

Life for everyone is colored by one's own attitudes. Touring Jerusalem and the rest of Israel reminds us of the reasons we live here and reinforces our commitment to maintain Israel as the Jewish homeland. I hope that as many of you as are able pick yourselves up and come to visit Israel. Jerusalem is a great place to start your visit!

NOT JUST FORESTS - THE JEWISH NATIONAL FUND

The JNF (Jewish National Fund) is familiar to most Jews, most notably for planting trees in Israel. The organization is known in Israel as the Keren Kayemeth LeIsrael, or KKL. While the forests that cover significant swaths of land here are the symbol of the JNF-KKL, they are certainly not its only important function. Today, while forestry is still important, the primary purpose of the Fund is to build Israel's infrastructure for environmental quality. (www.kkl.org.il)

In the forward to "Seed and Deed", Izi Mann's book celebrating the one hundredth anniversary of the Fund, a brief summation of the first century of the Fund appears: "How to condense in a few words the mission of redeeming a land of a people returning home, of planting forests on a scale of 220 million trees, of building 115 water reservoirs, restoring and reviving rivers, developing hundreds of recreation areas and parks, reclaiming land for some 1,000 communities, rolling back the desert, carving out thousands of kilometers of roads and bringing Zionist education to the entire Jewish diaspora?" These are just some of the miracles that resulted from our forefathers' vision and the little blue and white collection tins that were a familiar sight in many Jewish homes and businesses.

The JNF's era of land accumulation was climaxed in 1947 by the inclusion of the Negev Desert in the Jewish sector, as delineated by the UN Partition Plan. This highly significant breakthrough helped Israel successfully defend the Negev during the War of Independence, by legitimizing Jewish settlements there. Octogenarian Yoel De Malach, who was one of the founders of

Kibbutz Revivim, told this story: In the 1940s, it wasn't known if agriculture could flourish in the desert. Kibbutz Revivim became a pioneer in drip irrigation and the use of brackish water to grow plants. They were so successful that when the UN Commission visited there in 1947 and saw the pomegranates, dates, olives and flowers, they couldn't believe their eyes. "One of the UN officials walked out into a field of gladiolas, pulled a plant out by the roots, and checked it carefully. Then he pulled out several more plants. He thought it was a trick, that the flowers had been brought in for the occasion. Finally, they recommended that the Negev be included in Israel." (From an article by Yocheved Miriam Russo.)

Recently, we went on a tour of JNF projects in our region. We met licensed tour guide Neil Eisenstadt at Kibbutz Yad Hanna, which was named for Hanna Senesh. Senesh was a hero of WWII, who parachuted behind enemy lines to help the Allied war effort, but was caught and executed by the Nazis. We saw the kibbutz water treatment plant, built by the Fund at a cost of $40 million, which purifies polluted water draining into the area from the adjacent Palestinian-controlled areas. One of our group asked Neil whether the water was intentionally polluted by the Palestinians. He replied: No, but it is highly polluted with heavy industrial waste and untreated sewage. The Palestinians have received ample funding from donor nations to alleviate this situation, but much of the money has been diverted from that purpose.

We continued on to the Emeq Hefer Reclamation Plant, one of many that the Fund has constructed throughout Israel. Neil explained how the Fund builds the infrastructure necessary to maintain Israel's growing population and development activities. For example, the Fund built the reclamation plant for the Emeq

Hefer Regional Council, which resulted in increased development of the area's resources. It is the council's job, as it is in most Fund projects, to take responsibility for maintaining the infrastructure once it is turned over to them. We also noticed an undeveloped archeological site near the plant, which the Fund intends to restore, as it has with similar sites. A good example is the ancient Shuni fortress near Benyamina, which is surrounded by a beautiful park, hosts fairs and concerts, and has an excellent restaurant.

All over Israel parks and green areas have been built and developed by the Fund. These gardens and forests have opened up the countryside to all Israelis, who love to get out of town and set up barbecues on any occasion. We've been to many beaches, archeological sites, visitors' hospitality areas at army bases, and wooded areas where access has been improved by the Fund's efforts. Equally important are the Fund's continued infrastructure construction projects. The Fund often steps in when emergency measures are needed and governmental procedures are too slow. Currently, one of the Fund's biggest contributions is in reservoir building: 115 have been built in the 1990s alone. With the help of the Fund, Israel is belatedly tackling its significant water shortage problems.

While the Negev Desert constitutes 60% of Israel's territory, only 7% of the population lives there. Unfortunately, except for the large metropolis of Beersheva, Jews are vastly outnumbered by Beduin inhabitants in the Negev. The Fund's plan for settlements there works hand in hand with the government's road and rail projects to try to redress this problem. The goal of the Fund's vital "Blueprint Negev" is to significantly develop and settle empty parts of the Negev Desert.

Our guide remarked, "What would we Jews have done if the Jewish National Fund hadn't bought the land?" He's right. When the first Zionists embarked on their quest to repopulate our ancient land in the 19th century, the Turks were in control. Soon after, they were succeeded by the British. Neither was particularly hospitable to Jewish efforts to settle here. But because the Jewish National Fund / Keren Kayemeth LeIsrael had acted on its vision to resettle Jews in the Land of Israel and had purchased the land necessary for settlements, enough Jews came to make a difference.

Without a substantial start to immigration by the time of WWI, there would have been no Balfour Declaration. Without the Fund's help in combating the Arab Revolt before WWII, we might have succumbed to Arab violence, which was (at best) unhindered by the British. And without the Fund's efforts to assist the hundreds of thousands of Jews who streamed into Israel in the late 1940s and early 1950s, the Jewish enterprise in the Land of Israel might have floundered. The forests planted, the roads and trails constructed, the parcels of land redeemed, drained or reclaimed, the many communities built, the ancient sites restored, the modern water and sewage projects constructed - all of these are testaments to the vision of the early Zionists.

One of the Fund's great leaders, Dr. Joseph Weitz - known as "the father of the forests" for his years of dedication to reforesting the land - quoted Isaiah's prophecy of restoration in one of his own speeches: "Shout O heavens for the Lord has acted; Shout aloud, O depths of the earth! Shout for joy, O mountains, O forests with all your trees. For the Lord has redeemed Jacob, has gloried Himself through Israel." (Isaiah 44:23)

HIKING THE JUDEAN MOUNTAINS

We began our ESRA hike at Kibbutz Tsuba, close to the (Christian) Israeli-Arab town of Abu Ghosh. On the western side of the Jerusalem Mountains and close to Jerusalem, Abu Ghosh is known for both its excellent Middle Eastern-style restaurants and its many churches. On Saturdays, the town is often packed with Israelis enjoying humus, pita, and the many "oriental" food offerings. At certain times of the year, the town attracts large crowds who come to hear concerts performed in some of the picturesque churches. During the 1948 War of Independence, the townspeople of Abu Ghosh allied themselves with the Jews.

Our hike began on the other side of Route 1, at Kibbutz Tsuba. Our excellent guide, Avishai, related the modern history of the highway, which is known as the Tel Aviv-Jerusalem road. Its final route was set after the Six Day War of 1967, when the Jordanian Arab Legion was dislodged from the Latrun Fortress at the base of the Judean Mountains approaching Jerusalem. The kibbutz is located on the site of an Arab village of the same name. It was built by Israeli fighters and their families in 1948, after the defeat of the Egyptian and local Arab fighters during battles for control of the nearby Jerusalem highway.

It is thought that the Arab village was itself built on the remains of a Jewish one, which was settled after the defeat of a Canaanite tribe named Zobah, mentioned in 1 Samuel 14/47: "Now when Saul had taken his place as ruler of Israel, he made war on those who were against him on every side, Moab and the Ammonites and Edom and the kings of Zobah [also spelled Tsuba, Tzuba, or Suba] and the Philistines: and whichever way he went, he overcame them." This serial rebuilding - after military conquest - of villages which retained ancient, similar names, is common.

After a steep but short climb towards Tsuba, we stopped at the Belmont (Beautiful Mountain) Fortress to learn about the Crusader interlude in Palestine, which was first instigated by Pope Urban II in 1095, to rid Anatolia (modern Turkey) of Muslims. After a short time, taking Jerusalem and the Holy Land from the Muslims and freeing the Eastern Orthodox Christians became the primary goal of the Crusaders. Jerusalem was captured in 1099 and the Kingdom of Jerusalem and other Crusader "states" were established. This area of the Middle East, along the Mediterranean coast, had first come under Islamic rule in the 7th century, when followers of Mohammed surged westward out of the Arabian Desert, replacing the Byzantine Christian rulers who had succeeded the Roman governors.

Avishai explained the Arab perspective on the Crusaders, who are looked upon as barbarians who forced their culture onto the indigenous population, and who had a totally different way of life, language, religion – and personal hygiene. This viewpoint results in the Arabs describing Jews as "Crusaders". There is perhaps some validity to this, but the same could obviously be said about the Arabs themselves, in relation to the Jews and other residents of 7th century Palestine whom the Arabs conquered.

After leaving behind the ruins of the fortress and the later Arab village, we descended eastwards through the fields of Kibbutz Tsuba to a small valley full of fruit trees. We continued down Mt. Eitan through the ruins of the Arab village of Sataf, which is an ancient agricultural site in the Judean hills, not far from the Jerusalem neighborhood of Ein Karem.

We followed the path from the upper entrance to Sataf down to the Sorek river-bed, where there are pleasant orchards watered by two springs, one of which flows from a small cave nearby. It's fascinating that the orchards are grown according to the rules of ancient agriculture, with multiple terraces on the steep slope of the hill. There are some old buildings of yellow stone near the springs and the view of almond trees in bloom is fabulous. There are also large caves which were part of the irrigation system.

The 250-acre site is maintained by the Jewish National Fund and all the work is done by hand, or with the help of farm animals, without any machinery or use of pesticides. The site dates back to a Bronze Age village of 4,000 BCE, though most of the ruins are from the Byzantine era. The Arab villagers from Sataf were defeated in the War of Independence, after which there was a short-lived settlement of North African immigrants in that area.

"In 1985, the JNF began the restoration of ancient agricultural practices in the area, with the help of JNF supporters from Switzerland. The primary crops in the Judean Hills in ancient times included vineyards, olives, figs and pomegranates. In this rocky-hilly region, dry farming (which relies only on rainfall for irrigation) was practiced using an elaborate system of terraces and tunnels. The springs here were not plentiful, so the existing water supply had to be maximized. This was achieved by tunneling into the water-bearing strata. An ingenious system of channels (parts of which are clearly visible) conducted the water that was stored in large pools to the terraced plots. Sataf includes a 'prototype' vineyard including 26 ancient types of vines that were known to have grown in Eretz Israel." (www.gemsinisrael.com)

Avishai told us all about this area as we enjoyed our lunch, sitting in the shade of trees, with a massive wall built of boulders towering over us. He explained how deforestation and fluctuating population (sometimes there weren't enough people to maintain the agriculture) led to the destruction of the terraces and the resulting loss of soil. We then began the climb to Moshav Even Sapir, noticing how the huge terrace we had rested on had been formed by the construction of the rock wall. The drop from the top of the wall to the level terrace at its bottom was dramatic.

The moshav had been named for Pinchas Sapir, an Israeli pioneer who worked tirelessly to attract foreign investments by personally encouraging businessmen from the Diaspora to invest in Palestine and the nascent Jewish state. From there, we had a challenging uphill walk which included a short stint of rock climbing. We eventually reached a path winding past ancient springs and irrigation systems to the JNF picnic site in the Amminadav Forest. From there we had another shorter, uphill climb to the Kennedy Memorial.

The memorial, built shortly after the assassination of the young American president, is a circular building with emblems of all the American states. It is reminiscent of the trunk of a tree which has been cut off, symbolizing the shortened life of America's storybook president. From this point, we could look across a vista of mountains and valleys back to our starting point. It was the perfect conclusion to a wonderful day.

THE JEWISH PEOPLE LIVES! - YAD VASHEM

The Jewish people lives! *(Am Yisrael Chai!)* is a saying that is often heard in Israel, meaning that we have endured for thousands of years and that we will continue to endure forever. We were strongly reminded of this fact recently, when we visited Yad Vashem, the Holocaust Martyrs' and Heroes' Remembrance Authority in Jerusalem. Yad Vashem recently opened its Holocaust History Museum, a replacement for the original museum. It's situated on Mt. Herzl, adjacent to the national cemetery and the new Herzl Museum. Since we have previously spent time at the other venues on Yad Vashem's campus – such as the Valley of the Communities and the Children's Memorial – on this visit we concentrated on the new facility.

The architecture of the museum is striking: a 180 meter (600 feet) long triangular "spike" cutting through Mt Herzl with only its top, a skylight, visible above the mountain ridge. Designed by world-famous Israeli-born architect Moshe Safdie, the museum covers more than 40,000 square feet. After entering via a long, narrow shaft, your journey begins with the years preceding the Holocaust, immersing the visitor first in the atmosphere of European Jewry and then in the nightmare of the 1930s and 1940s. After visiting the first few galleries, placed on alternate sides of the central shaft, we realized that once entered, there is no "escape" from the museum. Each gallery leads across the shaft to the next, while the central passage is blocked by wire cable between the galleries, inhibiting a quick exit from the museum space. This is not a museum that encourages a superficial walkthrough.

While the multi-sensory experiences and the historical artifacts are nearly overwhelming, what really rivets one's attention are the filmed testimonies of the individual victims, some of whom appear multiple times in different galleries. These singular experiences make the museum immensely moving and unforgettable.

One survivor, who entered the camps at age 15, described how his philosophy of the law of the jungle helped him to survive. He figured out that only the strong could hope to endure in this hell, so he steeled himself to be one of the strongest, however high the cost. He narrated a few of the consequences which this fervor generated. The young man knew that in the morning roll-call the places safest from the guards and kapos (sadistic inmates who collaborated with the guards) were in the center of the second or third rows. To get one of those coveted positions, he sometimes had to elbow out someone else. There were deadly consequences for those who were pushed to the front.

During the roll-call, everyone had to wear his cap or face death. When his own cap was stolen, he snuck out of bed in the middle of the night and stole another's cap, which a fellow inmate had carelessly left peeking out from his bedclothes. At the roll-call the next morning, when he heard the crack of the shot which killed the unlucky cap-less prisoner, he didn't look to see who it was, for fear that the dead man's face would haunt him for the rest of his life.

Even more distressing was this survivor's regret that he failed to help his father to get up from the ground when he fell victim to the debilitating conditions. He let his father lie there because he knew the penalty for helping another prisoner was usually a bullet in the head. Five decades later, he still felt overwhelmed by guilt because of his failure to assist his father, although the older man would have perished anyway within a few days.

Another poignant story was told by the older brother of Israel Meir Lau. This young man, descended from more than two dozen generations of rabbis, had a job in a protected military industry when the Germans began to transfer the Jews to the concentration camps. To his chagrin, his father, following a biblical example, insisted that the family split itself up, the better to ensure that someone would survive to carry on the family name. Eventually, the older brother, a teenager, was taken to the camps along with his mother and five year old brother. The mother pushed the youngster into his older brother's unwilling arms, while the youngster struggled to remain with her. But, in a moment she was gone. The older brother took on the responsibility to somehow protect his sibling and miraculously, they both survived the camps. The pride and gratitude on the older brother's face was unmistakable as he described the children and grandchildren of his younger brother, who was able to carry on the family's rabbinical dynasty and to become Chief Rabbi of Israel.

A third survivor whose story greatly affected me was a woman, a teenager when she entered the camps. After being liberated, she found herself totally alone, with no surviving family. She met another survivor who was also alone and they quickly wed, which was not uncommon in the "rehabilitated" Displaced Persons camps where the Allies put the survivors after the war. But when she found out she was pregnant, the young wife was devastated that she might bring a child into the world. She narrated how she had heard so many crying babies during the war and had seen so much death that she wanted to prevent the baby's birth. Because she didn't have the money to pay for an abortion, she put a very hot cloth over her stomach and ironed her belly to try to abort the fetus. When that failed she tried lifting the heaviest objects that she could, to no avail. Finally, the baby was born, a son. When she held him in her arms, she prayed to God that he would live and thanked Him for giving her a son. Having a child turned out to be the catalyst that enabled her to begin a fruitful life, despite the horror that she had lived through.

In the next section of the museum, we learned about the illegal immigration to the Land of Israel, which often resulted in interment in Cyprus by the British, who still controlled the Mandate of Palestine after WWII. Along with personal narratives, we saw Ben-Gurion speak to the nation, declaring the establishment of the modern State of Israel. We also saw pictures of the ecstatic crowds expressing their joy over the announcement. At the end of the shaft, the last gallery in the museum is the Hall of Names, a repository for the Pages of Testimony of millions of Holocaust victims, and a memorial to those who perished. Beyond the hall is a room where visitors can conduct searches of the Shoah (Holocaust) Victims' Names Database. The circular repository contains the Pages of Testimony for each individual collected so far, with space for the entire six million pages in total. There are currently more than three million individual records in the database.

As people walk through the museum, they notice a gradual descent into the mountain. But when they approach the northern exit, the floor begins to ascend and the triangular shaft opens up again, with the exit bursting forth from the mountain's slope. The dramatic view of Jerusalem symbolizes the vitality of modern Israel, which came after – if not partially resulting from – the horror of the Holocaust. While we Israelis sometimes waver, our hope is that we retain enough of the strength that helped many of our people survive the Nazis' attempts to annihilate us. Even today, we need all our strength to repel the current attempts to disparage and destroy Israel and to erase the power and influence which our tiny, worldwide Jewish community has amassed.

JERUSALEM - CITY OF GOLD

The nickname for Jerusalem is the City of Gold. We understood the reference perfectly on a recent Saturday afternoon visit there. The sun reflected gold off the pinkish Jerusalem stone which covers all the buildings (by law) and the abundant greenery, after the winter rains, accented the city's rolling hills and valleys. Some buildings nestle in their proper places, like the Israel Museum, while others make bold architectural statements, like the YMCA.

While we and our friends aren't Sabbath-observant, we refrain from shopping on Shabbat, preferring to relax at home, visit friends, hike, go to a movie or a concert, or – best of all – ascend to Jerusalem, as they say in Hebrew. Jerusalem is one of the highest locations in Israel, about 3,000 feet above sea level, but it seems even higher because its eastern sectors overlook the Judean Desert, which slopes down to 1,300 feet below sea level at the Dead Sea.

On this visit we first went to the Israel Museum, an architectural and landscape gem. The museum consists of several distinct but connecting pavilions which fit snugly into the hills of the museum district of the city, where the Knesset and the Supreme Court are also located. Perhaps the Israel Museum's most distinctive feature is the detached building which contains the Dead Sea Scrolls. Its roof is shaped like the wicker cover of a basket, not unlike the basket which once contained the Dead Sea scrolls themselves. The striking, white-tiled roof is continuously sprinkled with streams of water, which is part of the cooling system protecting the ancient scrolls.

On our previous outing to the museum (we are members and go frequently) we saw an exhibit about Boris Schatz and the Bezalel art school and museum, which was the precursor to the modern Israel Museum. This time we saw a remarkable, large exhibit and a smaller, but more intimate one. The main exhibit was of South American origin, the first comprehensive exhibition ever devoted to the Chimu culture: Imperial Riches from the Desert of Peru. This fantastic display offered a portrait of daily life and aristocratic splendor in the capital city of the Chimu civilization of Peru (1100–1470 CE), the largest empire to control the Andean desert coast before the rise of the Incas. We saw more than 200 objects from the Israel Museum's rich holdings and from private collections: gold and silver works, textiles and featherwork, shell jewelry, and ceramics, as well as burial offerings from the tomb of a Chimu lord.

The second exhibit was The Botanist's Brush: Shmuel Charuvi's Drawings for the Hareuveni Floral Treasury of the Land of Israel. This is a collection of exquisite drawings for a planned botanical encyclopedia of the Land of Israel, painted between 1923 and 1927 by the painter Shmuel Charuvi. Under the guidance of botanists Ephraim and Hannah Hareuveni, Charuvi reproduced the Land of Israel's plant life, demonstrating a fantastic technique with unusual detailing. Although the Treasury never became a reality, more than 35 watercolors were preserved intact by the Hareuveni family. We were thrilled to see examples of the many varieties which grow right in our own neighborhood.

Afterwards, we looked for a restaurant serving a late lunch. While in Tel Aviv and other Israeli cities many restaurants and cafés are open on Shabbat, in Jerusalem it's the opposite. We finally decided to dine at the restaurant at the YMCA, the complex that sits opposite the King David Hotel and is easily its equal in architectural splendor. Designed in 1933 by the same architect who built the Empire State Building a few years earlier, the Y-complex is a magnificent landmark of Jerusalem, distinguished especially by its high clock tower (with a fantastic view of the Old City), its unique interiors, and its spacious courtyards.

Following our tasty and inexpensive meal in a cozy indoor dining room, we picked a tour from our book, "Jerusalem – a walk through time" by Yad Ben-Zvi. This two-volume set includes walking tours of ancient Jerusalem, the Ottoman and Mandate periods, and the modern city. We settled on a walk through the nearby Talbieh neighborhood into the Katamon district. Highlights of the walk were the Belgian Embassy on Salameh Circle, named for the original Arab merchant who built the beautiful home there, many other nearby Arab mansions built after WWI, and the modern Jerusalem Theater at the end of the same street, constructed on land donated by the wealthy Sherover family (who also paid for a fabulous promenade and park which overlooks the Old City).

On the way back to our car we had a mini-adventure, navigating the practically unlit park near the Jerusalem Theater in the dark, which was almost scary. We drove back to the museum district to the Bible Lands Museum, whose simple architectural design wisely doesn't try to compete with the Israel Museum located just opposite. The Bible Lands Museum was founded by the late Dr. Elie Borowski, a former yeshiva student who was a WWII fighter in a Polish unit of the French Army and later became a renowned Middle Eastern scholar and collector. The museum contains an incredible array of material depicting biblical history through ancient Near Eastern art and artifacts, from the dawn of civilization through the early Christian era. In addition, the museum presents Saturday night concerts nearly every week.

After spending a brief time viewing some of the exhibits, we went downstairs to enjoy the wine and cheese spread that precedes the concerts, hearing a mixture of Hebrew, French, and English from the crowd. We enjoyed the accomplished American-Israeli singer, Adina Friedman, who did renditions of songs made famous by Billie Holiday, Roberta Flack, and many others.

By 10:30 that evening we were on our way back home, less than an hour away. For us, Shabbat is one of the best things about living in Israel. While we know that enjoying Shabbat is an option available to all Jews, in the Diaspora Shabbat is appreciated mostly by Orthodox Jews. For non-observant Jews, the frenetic seven-day-a-week shopping and everyday activities are too much of a distraction and Shabbat is practically overlooked. But in Israel, most of the population slows down considerably on Shabbat and enjoys a day of relaxation, or an activity different from the work week. We arrived home late, but very satisfied from our eventful day in Jerusalem, the City of Gold.

BIALIK STREET, TEL AVIV

Chaim Nachman Bialik was born in the Ukraine in 1873 and later became known as Israel's "national poet". Bialik was most famous for his two poems about the Kishinev pogroms in Russia. The second poem, "Be-Ir ha-Haregah" ("In the City of Slaughter," 1904), was a searing denunciation of the Jews' meek submission to the massacre, in which Bialik is bitter at the absence of justice and struck by the world's indifference - and even the indifference of nature: "The sun shone, the acacia blossomed, and the slaughterer slaughtered." This poem resonated with the Zionist feelings of Jews, especially those living in Eastern Europe and, of course, those who had immigrated to Palestine.

Our guide Yona described Bialik's sojourn in Palestine to a group of us at the corner of the street named for him in Tel Aviv. In 1924, fifteen years after the founding of the first modern Jewish city, Tel Aviv, Bialik and his wife left Berlin after a three year stay. Upon arriving in Tel Aviv they were given a splendid reception by Mayor Meir Dizengoff, a friend of the poet, who informed them that a street was to be named in the poet's honor.

At that time the growing city was a collection of village-like neighborhoods consisting mostly of one-story houses. Though the population barely reached 17,000, Tel Aviv was already full of contagious excitement. The Fourth Aliyah (wave of immigration) was just beginning. Most of the new immigrants were middle-class and brought with them modest sums of capital with which they established small businesses and workshops. It was during this period that Tel Aviv began its transformation into a real metropolis.

We strained to hear Yona's commentary above the din of the traffic and loud conversation at the adjacent café, which occupied the site of one of Tel Aviv's earliest gathering spots. It was hard to imagine that when Dizengoff and Bialik had stood here so long ago, there were no buildings blocking the view of the beach. In fact, sand dunes surrounded them and donkeys and camels were common beasts of burden. Yona soon led us down the short street towards Beit Bialik (Bialik House), describing the architecture of the buildings and telling stories about many of their inhabitants.

Beginning in 1924 and continuing until the end of the decade, the style of building in Tel Aviv was "Eclectic", a classical architecture with oriental features such as arched windows with Jewish ceramic motifs. Because there was no "Jewish architecture", the builders added biblical figures and Jewish symbols to the columns and arches to create a Jewish feeling. A number of the oldest original houses on Bialik Street were in the Eclectic style, many with ornamental ponds in their gardens. Yona told us that the inhabitants, many of whom had homes without baths, would put live carp in these ponds shortly before the Sabbath. Later these carp were to be clubbed on the head and made into gefilte fish.

During the 1930s there was a huge German influence on the burgeoning city's architecture, from Palestinian (Jews born in Palestine) architects who studied in Germany and from new immigrants who fled Germany and Europe to practice architecture in Tel Aviv. Approximately 4,500 buildings were designed by more than 60 architects in the International Style, which in Tel Aviv was called "Bauhaus", after the famous German design school of the same name in Dessau, Germany. We saw many of these on Bialik Street. This simple, unembellished style was designed within a social context, primarily for the working class. Because thousands of these buildings, usually painted white, are still standing - the majority in great need of extensive renovation - Tel Aviv is called the White City and has been accorded the status of UNESCO World Heritage Site. (Most of the International Style buildings in Europe were destroyed during WWII.)

Due to Tel Aviv's Mediterranean climate, the architects made adjustments to the International Style buildings, adding deep, rounded balconies, flat roofs, and smaller, horizontal windows to cut the glare of the Mediterranean sun. The exteriors were whitewashed with either smooth or rough plaster over bricks. The idea was to build an apartment that would be cool in summer and comfortably warm in the winter. Therefore, the living rooms generally faced west and the bedrooms faced east. The apartment units themselves were quite small and the inhabitants spent much of their time on the balconies, which sometimes had modifications to increase the circulation of ocean breezes.

After Israel's independence in 1948, the newly independent state was inundated with immigrants from European and Arab countries. The Bauhaus style was overtaken by a simpler, cheaper type of construction which could be quickly mass-produced, called "blokim". Similar to the Bauhaus buildings, blokim were built on pillars one level above ground for circulation and additional public space. The space for balconies was enclosed to enlarge the living room/dining area and the apartments were usually given glass sliding walls on the street side, with plastic shutters to control the shade. There was only one of this type building on upscale Bialik Street, but it had been "dressed up" with glazed tile to attempt to fit in with its more fancy neighbors.

It took us quite a while to traverse the short street to its end at Kikar Bialik (Bialik Square) due to all the explanations and stories that Yona told. Around the square are the street's most significant buildings: the Rueven Rubin Museum (once the home of one of Israel's most beloved painters), Museum of the History of Tel Aviv-Jaffa (once the home of Mayor Dizengoff and later the City Hall), the Felicia Blumenthal Music Center Auditorium (located in a beautiful former factory), the Bauhaus Museum (a small furniture exhibit located in a beautifully restored apartment house), and the ultimate goal of our tour, Beit Bialik.

Chaim Nachman Bialik was already a famous poet, acclaimed as the "national poet", before he moved to the Yishuv. In 1923, while still in Europe and on the jubilee of his birth, Bialik created a sumptuous four-volume set of his poetry which proved to be extremely successful. This provided him with the funds to build a fabulous house for himself and his wife on "his" street.

Bialik's house, designed by Y. Minor, is an outstanding example of the synthesis of European architecture with an Arab decorative motif. "Arches and columns beautify every corner of the house; in the oriental custom the roof was built flat to allow for a pleasant place to while away hot summer evenings, with a view of the city under construction; the windows of the building are low, as a protection against the harsh sun. The most obvious oriental element is the tower topped by a dome. The hearth and the pillars are covered with decorated tiles, with Jewish themes, products of the Bezalel [famous artistic] workshop in Jerusalem." The dedication of the building took place during the festival of Succot, 1925. (www.mfa.gov.il)

Ironically, Bialik didn't write poetry while living in his new home, but he did translation and other work there and had a sort of salon for all the well-known literary, scientific, Zionist and other luminaries who wouldn't think of visiting Tel Aviv without stopping in at Beit Bialik. Tel Aviv was the logical place for the famous poet to reside, because to Bialik and others, Tel Aviv represented the home for the new Jew, the replacement for the "old" Jew who had been a victim and scapegoat for so long. But in 1933 the social pressures of being so famous proved to be too much for the elderly couple and the Bialiks moved to a smaller place in the Tel Aviv suburb of Ramat Gan. Sadly, the next year Bialik traveled to Vienna for an operation, where he died.

Tel Aviv is indeed a city for the new Jew, and is a wonderful counterweight to Jerusalem, Israel's most famous city. Lively Tel Aviv always has innumerable events to keep its residents and visitors busy. We enjoyed our walk down this short street so full of the city's history. Before leaving Bialik Street, we enjoyed lunch at the same location where Tel Aviv residents have dined for more than 85 years. But we had only a glimpse of the sea due to the continuous construction over the last century, which perhaps Chaim Bialik and Mayor Dizengoff foresaw on that day of welcome in 1924.

EXPLORING ANCIENT JERUSALEM

Jerusalem is a treasure trove of exciting experiences for those interested in the history of monotheism, the Jewish people, the Middle East, and contemporary culture. During a recent visit to this globally significant city, my wife and I explored two sites which pertain to Jerusalem's ancient history and its impact on contemporary Jews. The first on our list was the Rockefeller Archaeological Museum, close to the Old City walls in east Jerusalem.

Built in the 1930s outside of the northeast corner of the Old City, the Rockefeller Museum was then strictly a British project. Having gathered a collection of wonderful archeological finds dating from prehistoric times to the Ottoman period (which ended in 1917), the British set about finding a benefactor to fund the first archeological museum in Palestine. They turned to the American philanthropist John D. Rockefeller, Jr. for the initial funding. Rockefeller donated two million dollars, an enormous sum for that era, to build what was officially named the Palestine Archaeological Museum (but was commonly called the Rockefeller Museum).

The museum is a standout example of the fusion of Western and oriental architectural traditions, with modern innovations. It was designed by the architect Austen St. Barbe Harrison, who had previously been employed by the government of Greece to design and renovate buildings in Macedonia, where he studied Byzantine and Islamic architecture. Appointed Chief Architect of the Mandatory Department of Public Works in 1922, Harrison built numerous public buildings in Jerusalem. The museum was completed in 1938.

During the period Jordan occupied east Jerusalem (1948-1967), King Hussein nationalized the museum, which had heretofore been run by an international board of trustees. Israel gained control of all of Jerusalem during the Six Day War of 1967 and affiliated the Rockefeller Museum with the burgeoning Israel Museum. Since then, new archeological finds have gone to the Israel Museum, a much larger facility.

There is free admission to the museum but no parking nearby. The permanent exhibition is arranged in a chronological display of the history of the Holy Land. The rare objects on display are archeological markers of Israel's history. All the exhibits were discovered in the Land of Israel from the 1920s into the 1940s, though other, temporary exhibitions dealing with a variety of subjects can be accommodated. Harrison's design is somewhat old-fashioned, which is part of the museum's charm. There are five main rooms, including two of octagonal shape, surrounding the wonderful, cloistered Central Court. All the rooms benefit from high windows which provide natural lighting for the exhibits.

The museum's most striking architectural features are the three story octagonal tower at the entrance and the striking blue-tiled prayer niche facing the pool in the courtyard. The niche was designed by Armenian artist David Ohanessian, who was originally brought to Jerusalem to make repairs to the tile work at the Dome of the Rock. He was the first of a wave of Armenian tile artists to come to Jerusalem. (Their legacy is the many Armenian tile shops in Jerusalem.) Other outstanding design features of the museum include ten wall reliefs in the courtyard, designed by British artist Eric Gill, representing the major civilizations that influenced the cultural life of the region; another larger relief of Gill's located above the museum entrance; and elegantly engraved and painted English, Hebrew, and Arabic inscriptions on the museum walls. It was interesting to learn that the Jordanians hid the Hebrew inscriptions during the time they controlled the museum. (For more information see: www.english.imjnet.org.il)

Our next stop is so popular that it must be booked weeks ahead: the fabulous Western Wall tunnel, located next to the Western Wall. Formerly called the Wailing Wall, the Western Wall is a remnant of the western retaining wall of the Temple Mount, which was conceived by King David and built by his son, King Solomon, about 1,000 BCE. The Western Wall tunnel provides the closest proximity to the location of the vanished Ark of the Covenant. As an indication of the reverence that the site enjoys, every day people of all nationalities, races, and faiths congregate at the Wall to pray, contemplate, or perhaps just to place a written message to the Supreme Being in its cracks.

The 187-foot length of the Wall that is visible in the Western Wall Plaza is just a fraction of the entire Wall, which is 1,600 feet in length. There are 45 levels (courses) of stone work, 28 of them above ground, and the remaining 17 underground! It is only since 1967, when Israel regained control of the Old City, that Jews have had access to the tunnels and the ability to discover and renovate previously hidden areas. Because of the efforts of the Ministry of Religious Affairs, the entire length of the Western Wall has now been revealed by the tunnel excavations. Discoveries include many rooms, public halls, a section of a Second Temple road, a Hasmonean water tunnel, a pool, incredible arches which support the various levels of construction, and more.

A sense of awe overwhelms most visitors as they are guided through the tunnels, especially at the section that is only three hundred feet from where the Ark of the Covenant - the Holy of Holies - once rested. (The current location of the ark is a mystery which continues to arouse speculation.)

The sizes of the stones used to construct the tunnels range from relatively small to a gargantuan stone more than 40-feet long. The stone courses that are underground, as well as some above ground, are the original Western Wall stones from the time of Herod the Great, more than 2,000 years old. Other stones were placed on top of them during later eras: Roman, Crusader, and Ottoman. While touring the tunnel, one can see excavations of lower levels from earlier periods, some of which are scores of feet below.

Midway through the tour we saw a short documentary about the methods the builders used in those days. Stonecutters used hammers, chisels and metal wedges to quarry the stones. To move them from the quarries the builders used large mechanical cranes with levers and pulleys and huge wheels or log rollers, which formed a type of conveyor belt. Once moved from their resting place, the stones were transported by oxen or even by "manpower".

The tour concluded at the terminus of a typical King Herod-era street, which was abruptly left unfinished upon Herod's death in 4 BCE. This was evident from the fact that we stood at a "dead end", which happens to be the location of the last stand of the

Jews against the Romans in 70 CE, when the Second Temple was razed.

Our excellent guide, Rivka, reminded us of the Prophet Zechariah's visions: "And the streets of the city shall be full of boys and girls playing in the streets thereof. And I will bring them, and they shall dwell in the midst of Jerusalem and they shall be my people, and I will be their God in truth and in righteousness." (Zechariah: 5/8) There we stood, youngsters and their parents or grandparents, walking on a street built by Herod more than 2,000 years ago, fulfilling Zechariah's prophecies. Only in Jerusalem!

PASSOVER ADVENTURES

This year my brother Charles had a great Passover in Israel. While every Jew who participates in a Seder (the festive Passover meal) repeats "Next year in Jerusalem!", very few who live outside of the Land of Israel actually come here to celebrate one of our most unique holidays. In America, for instance, the holiday is celebrated by most Jews at a Seder the first evening and a second one the following night. That's about it. What a difference here!

In Israel, everyone has a day off from work the first and last days of Passover and the intermediate days of the holiday are either vacation-time or half-days off for many workers. As usual, we celebrated the Seder at our close friends' house. We covered just about the entire Haggadah prayer booklet, ate a fabulous holiday feast, and then finished the Seder with its rousing, traditional songs. The next day we rested after the huge effort (mostly by my wife Michal) of making our house kosher for Passover. On Friday afternoon my brother arrived, in plenty of time to get ready for Shabbat dinner.

Our friends Jeremy and Chaya joined us for dinner along with our two sons. Following the meal we reviewed the plans for Charles' time here. While I believe that "missions" from America are a splendid way to visit Israel, especially for first-timers, I encourage visitors to try a less structured trip (at least after their initial visit) so that they can spend more time doing what the locals do. For example, locals don't hear speakers from the Foreign Ministry or visit a community center for underprivileged immigrants. But we do lots of other interesting things that tourists usually have no time to discover.

On Shabbat, we went hiking with our usual crew, the Shochets and the Hararis. As we crossed the wide Ayalon Valley towards Jerusalem, our friend and unofficial guide, Shaike, told Charles about the history of this locale, site of so many great battles through the centuries. It was here that Joshua led the Israelites into battle against the Amorites, not long after the Jews entered the Land of Israel. Shaike explained how Joshua raised his arms to halt the travel of the sun across the heavens, prolonging the day and allowing the Israelites to vanquish their enemy: "'Stand still, O sun, at Gibeon, O moon, in the Valley of Ayalon!' And the sun stood still and the moon halted, while a nation wreaked judgment on its foes." (Joshua 10.12, 13)

We passed the Latrun Fort, now the Armored Corps Museum, and began the ascent into the Jerusalem hills. We quickly reached the Elah Valley where King Saul's army fought the Philistines. It was here that the young shepherd David volunteered to be Israel's champion to fight the giant Goliath. In those days, armies often used "champions" to fight as proxies for their respective armies. When none of the more experienced warriors were brave enough to face the giant, Saul had no choice but to send David against him. Refusing to wear armor and armed only with his slingshot and five smooth stones, David went forth and vanquished Goliath, whereupon the Philistines fled the battleground. Mindful of the historic setting, we parked and began our hike in the valley, outside the settlement of Mata, established in 1948. For several hours we hiked through the woodlands and made our way back to the car through expansive fields filled with wildflowers, quite off the beaten track.

Next, we went to the nearby Beit Guvrin National Park. We took the "short route" through the park, passing ancient olive oil presses, underground water cisterns, ornate burial caves, other caves with hundreds of niches to hold pigeons – which were raised to be sold as inexpensive sacrifices for the Temple in Jerusalem – and a reconstructed dwelling from nearly two thousand years ago. We saw the remains of an ancient Hellenistic town, Maresha, which had been conquered by a Maccabean king in 113 BCE, but was later lost to others in battle. Eventually the town was razed and over the centuries mounded by dirt (creating a tell), which archeologists eventually discovered and explored.

The next day we went to Jerusalem. During the holidays it is the custom to visit at least one of Israel's walled cities, of which Jerusalem is the most prominent. We had made reservations at the Herzl Museum in the afternoon, leaving us enough time to eat lunch in the city. We stopped at a typical Israeli "restocafé", where meals, alcoholic drinks, as well as coffee and tea are served. This particular café was the site of a horrific homicide bombing several years before. To their credit, the owners had rebuilt immediately and the café has continued to be a popular spot, especially for locals.

The Herzl Museum, an example of the new audio-visual style now common in Israel, was a great experience. We joined a group and were shunted through several rooms, each evoking a period and atmosphere from Theodor Herzl's life. An assimilated Jewish journalist living in Vienna, Herzl was so shocked during his reporting of the famous Dreyfus Affair in France that he became an almost-frenzied Zionist overnight. Within a few years he had powered the Zionist philosophy from near-obscurity to a worldwide Jewish (and to a lesser extent, Christian) movement. He convoked the first Zionist Congress in Basel with scores of delegates and used the growing movement as his starting point to build the Jewish State.

The museum's presentation was clever and entertaining, educating the audience who knew little about Herzl and extending the knowledge of those who were already familiar with his exploits. Herzl, who was crazy enough to predict the establishment of a modern Jewish state within the next fifty years (he was off by only one year!) literally wore his heart out in his constant visits to influential Christian and Ottoman Muslim leaders around the globe, trying to convince them of the value of a Jewish State in Palestine. He famously said, "If you will it, it is no dream." Without Herzl's efforts, modern Israel might not exist. Certainly, without him, it would have taken more than fifty-one years to be established.

Another day, Charles and I went to the seaside town of Netanya, where the FPF (Forgotten People Fund) is based. This grassroots charity run by friends of ours serves many Ethiopian immigrants in the Netanya area. While Israel has undertaken to bring in scores of thousands of Jews from Ethiopia, even extending a welcome to many of their relatives who had been forced to convert to Christianity decades before, life in Israel has not been wonderful for them, to say the least. The older generation, especially the men, have found themselves unable to cope with modern society due to a lack of spoken Hebrew and the incredible gulf between life in modern Israel and their previous lives in Africa. Most of the population lives below the poverty line. Hope for the future of these immigrants lies mostly with the children, many of whom are beginning to become comfortable in Israeli society. Meanwhile, the majority of Ethiopian families are in dire need of help.

We accompanied Anne Silverman of FPF while she distributed food vouchers to those families whom she couldn't reach before the Passover holiday began. We went to at least a half dozen apartments, most of which were neat and sparsely furnished, but all of which had TVs, cabinets, sofas, and beds. The children were somewhat shy, but there were plenty of sparks of humor and intelligence in their eyes, enough to repay Anne and her cohorts for their hard work and determination to help.

Nearly all the Ethiopian families live in apartments whose purchase has been subsidized by the government. But the mortgages, which are small, are a burden for their unemployed owners. One family, where extra help had been given to renovate their ground floor apartment, was particularly impressive. The parents and their twelve children now have a second bathroom, additional furniture, bedding, and other improvements courtesy of FPF. The youngsters we met were happily playing in the front yard enjoyed posing for a picture. To learn more about Ethiopians in Israel, go to www.fpf.org.il.

That afternoon we drove to Tel Aviv, to the Nahalat Binyamin section of the city, where there is a biweekly crafts fair in the pedestrian-only area. The trees were decorated with fanciful ornaments and the booths were filled with interesting and unusual items. The cafés were bustling, including the one where we enjoyed excellent Italian-style ice cream. We picked up some intriguing gifts and then went into the adjacent Carmel Market. The market, famous for its raucous vendors, was filled with shoppers buying all types of items, from food to music cassettes. We picked up what we needed and headed back home.

On the last day of Charles' visit, we drove to Modi'in, a planned city between Tel Aviv and Jerusalem. The town, which already has tens of thousands of residents, is sprouting new neighborhoods every year. A rapid train line will soon connect the city with Tel Aviv and Jerusalem (the Tel Aviv section is complete), which will accelerate growth even more. We visited friends originally from the Atlantic City area who reside there with their three young children. Being a fairly typical young family, both parents work, one in high-tech and one in education. With two incomes, young, educated couples like our friends are able to have a pleasant home and a nice lifestyle.

That evening, Charles, the boys and I went to Cinema City, a large cineplex with many shops and trendy eateries. We enjoyed a current movie and ate in one of the popular restaurants. As Charles said, "It could have been anywhere." Perhaps this is part of the debt we owe to Theodor Herzl. He wished the Jews to have "a state like all the others." Israel's dual challenge is to survive as a Jewish State which retains our rich cultural benefits while battling the negative characteristics which afflict so many states.

Passover is a fabulous time to tour Israel. If you haven't been to Israel yet, or it's been a long while since you visited, think about coming, either with a group or on your own!

ALL IN A DAY - JERUSALEM

Shabbat is usually a day of relaxation for us, but this past Shabbat was quite different. Michal and I attended a special bar mitzvah in the morning at our small Masorti (Conservative) congregation in Kohav Ya'ir, we saw a fascinating exhibit in Jerusalem at the Israel Museum, and we spent the evening in the city's Russian Compound.

It was a very special bar mitzvah that morning. Reina Nuernberger's grandson Ryan came from New Jersey, with family and friends, to celebrate his big day with our congregation. Many families bring their children to Israel for either their bar mitzvah, or a bar mitzvah trip, so Ryan's consecration was not unique – except for the fact that the Torah used in the service was rescued by his Grandfather Bill from his ancestral village in Austria.

Bill, who has since passed away, had returned to Austria many times since fleeing the country in 1938, shortly after Hitler's uncontested annexation of the country (the Anschluss). In 1980, Bill and his wife Reina were visiting his hometown, Steyr, where his father had been the rabbi of a congregation of about one hundred Jews. Unlike Bill, most of the local Jews had remained in the community and eventually perished in the Nazi death camps. Bill's parents were among the murdered, but his boyhood friend Fritz had survived. Fritz had reclaimed his family home in Steyr after the war, married a gentile, and rebuilt his life.

While visiting with Fritz, Bill and Reina were flabbergasted to see the congregation's Torah scroll. Only a few weeks before, Fritz had noticed a large trash container outside the home of the former town pharmacist, a Nazi leader during the war. Major renovations were being carried out by the new owner and the container was nearly full with "junk" from the house. For some reason Fritz peered into the container and discovered the Torah! He pulled it out and hurried home with his prize.

Fritz's wife objected to his bringing home "trash" and asked him to return it to the container, since it is against the law to forage through the trash in Austria. Fritz quickly explained to her the significance of his find and described how the Nazis of Steyr and their many sympathizers had desecrated the synagogue and stolen its contents on Kristallnacht (the Night of Breaking Glass), which was the Nazis' first major and widespread anti-Semitic action. Fritz retrieved the Torah just a half-hour before the trash truck arrived and emptied the container.

Bill and Reina were stunned to hear this miraculous story of how the Torah had reappeared after 42 years, virtually undamaged! They brought the Torah back to their home in Israel, where it assumed a place of honor and use in the main synagogue of Kohav Ya'ir. Our congregation borrowed the scroll for this auspicious occasion. It was very meaningful for us to hear this story and to use the rescued Torah at Ryan's bar mitzvah.

In the afternoon, we drove to Jerusalem to one of our favorite haunts, the Israel Museum. We had just enough time before closing to see a temporary exhibit as well as a new, permanent installation. The display in the Weisbord Pavilion, which is the venue for large, temporary exhibits, was "Bread: Daily and Divine". Though bread is an ordinary topic, the show was fascinating. Many different types of bread were showcased, mostly of a devotional variety. Of course, the largest selection was of Jewish challahs, the traditional braided loaf eaten on Shabbat. But Christian and Moslem breads were also featured, along with more mundane exhibits of "our daily bread".

Two things stood out. There was a film made of interviews with several Israeli bakers, ranging from the gentleman who created the first bread "factory" in the late 1920s, to the scion of one of the old-time bakery families, to the master baker who started the first boutique bakery here. Today, factory-baked loaves and pita bread are the mainstays, but one can also buy fabulous bread made by artisans who create bread the old-fashioned way.

The most mind-boggling exhibit was a crystallized, black lump. This turned out to be the last portion of bread saved by a prisoner at the Bergen Belsen concentration camp, from the day she was miraculously freed from the camp. It was totally unrecognizable as bread, but the elderly survivor proudly uses it as a centerpiece each year at her Seder (Passover meal) table, so that her children and grandchildren will appreciate the freedom that they enjoy today.

Later, after a snack at a café, we walked through the Russian Compound, which is near the Zion Square pedestrian mall. In the mid-nineteenth century, after their defeat by the Europeans and Ottoman Turks in the Crimean War, the Russians increased their holdings in Jerusalem. An area to the north of the Old City was purchased by the Grand Duke Constantine for the use of Russian Pilgrims. Large hospices, a church, a hospital, and other structures were built on what became known as the Russian Compound. As we walked through this picturesque neighborhood, sort of a miniature city, we passed the Sergei Hostel, named for Prince

Sergei, brother of Czar Alexander III. Built in 1890, it provided first and second-class accommodations and amenities for the Russian travelers. Just as we were passing the gate built into the substantial walls, the caretaker appeared. When we expressed interest in seeing the garden in the large courtyard, he insisted that we enter.

The garden, which the caretaker has tended for more than twenty years, is a beautiful spot for Jerusalemites to enjoy during the weekdays, when it is open from morning until night. We walked among the benches, tall trees and foliage, centuries-old stone wells, and ancient agricultural implements. Thanks to these antiquities, donated decades ago by General Moshe Dayan - who stole them in the Sinai Peninsula - the courtyard is an outdoor museum as well as a great place for a lunch break.

The most exciting part of our visit to the hostel was when the caretaker took us to one of the high turrets that anchor the building. We climbed to the top of a creaky, dirty spiral staircase, which was built around a giant timber brought all the way from Siberia. The view from the rooftop was magnificent. We had a 360 degree view of the entire city, all the way to the Moabite Mountains of Jordan. It was a fitting end to a busy day in Israel.

JERUSALEM NIGHTS

The Succot holiday has finished and Israel's six-month "rainy" season is just beginning. The eight-day festival (nine days in the Diaspora) ends with Simhat Torah, which celebrates the Jewish love affair with our holy scripture, the Torah. On two evenings during the intermediate days of Succot, we went up to Jerusalem to visit a few museums and to meander through the city.

We arrived at the Israel Museum minutes before 4 o'clock, just in time to join an English-language tour of the famous model of the city of Jerusalem in the Second Temple period. The model was built in the 1960s by the owner of the Holyland Hotel in honor of his son, who had died during the War of Independence. When the site of the hotel was recently sold and developed as a huge condominium complex, the grandson of the hotel owner contacted the Israel Museum to see whether it could accommodate the 1-acre miniature.

The museum had an empty one-acre plot adjacent to the Shrine of the Book complex, which houses the Dead Sea scrolls. Since the scrolls are of 1st century CE provenance and the model depicts Jerusalem of the same period, the museum jumped at the opportunity. The miniature "walled city" is connected to the scrolls complex by a beautiful garden walkway, along which one can see a film depicting Jerusalem in the year 66, just before the Romans conquered and sacked the city.

The model, disassembled into 1,000 pieces and rebuilt on the new site, was located so that people first see the model as if they were gazing on it from the Mount of Olives, which is often a tourist's first viewpoint of the Old City. Our excellent guide explained the most prominent sights as we walked around the miniature.

We saw both Robinson's Arch and Wilson's Bridge (both named after British archeologists) as they were originally constructed, connecting parts of Jerusalem to the Temple Mount, where the magnificent Second Temple stood. Completely rebuilt by Herod the Great, the Temple was crafted of local limestone (as buildings in Jerusalem are built even today) and was said to be the most magnificent project of the time. The Temple Complex is a relatively huge area, augmented by Herod's palace next to the outermost wall. From viewing the miniature one gets an unequalled perspective on Jerusalem at that time, including the three separate walls which were built at various periods in the city's history, progressively increasing Jerusalem's area.

We left the Israel Museum and went to the Tower of David Museum, which is located in the original Herod's Palace we had just seen in miniature. The Tower of David citadel has extensive exhibits depicting the history of the city of Jerusalem in innovative ways. But its real gem is the extensive courtyard, a perfect venue for special events, such as the show "Soundscapes" then showing, a visual and musical extravaganza.

The second evening was spent in Nahalat Shiva, the third community in Jerusalem constructed outside of the Old City walls. Dating back to 1869, the neighborhood was a cooperative effort built by seven Jerusalem families who pooled their funds to purchase the land and construct the first houses. Since the land was owned by a local Arab who despised Jews, the founders of Nahalat Shiva sent one of their daughters, disguised as an Arab, to buy the field and then register it in the Ottoman land office. The cost of the land left enough funds to build only one house, whose owner was decided by a lottery. Rabbi Yosef Rivlin was the winner and his was the first house in the neighborhood. One of the two main streets of Nahalat Shiva is named in Rabbi Rivlin's honor. (www.biu.ac.il)

In the 1960s, the Jerusalem municipality considered tearing down the two streets and the connecting alleys for urban renewal. Luckily, wiser heads prevailed. Today the neighborhood is a thriving one of shops, restaurants, and bars. The streets are usually crowded in the evenings with locals eating and drinking and tourists doing likewise, plus shopping in the many specialty shops which line the streets.

We had come to Jerusalem that evening for a nighttime succah tour, but our guide decided that we would walk around Nahalat Shiva instead. We soon found ourselves in a cozy courtyard, with a tiny, beautiful synagogue which Rabbi Rivlin had founded. This sanctuary, reminiscent of some of the synagogues in the holy city of Safed, is the second oldest one built outside of the Old City walls. There was a small succah nearby so we went over to check it out. While talking to its owner, our guide discovered that for a few years, decades ago, he had lived in our hometown!

Our Succot holiday this year was great. In Israel, fall and spring are the best times of year to come. I'm sure that my readers would really enjoy a trip here at this time or during Passover, which often coincides with Easter. Of course, we Israelis would appreciate your visit. Not to mention - you'll have a fabulous time!

WINTER HIKE NEAR BEIT SHEMESH

Israel had a nearly dry autumn this year, but winter thankfully began with a major rainstorm. That means muddy boots for hikers! About a dozen of us, mostly members of my wife Michal's hiking club, headed to British Park for an outing. On the roads through the rolling hills, we encountered many groups of bike riders who have made this area one of Israel's favorite attractions for bikers.

The British Park / Park Brittania, in the heart of the Judean Plain, covers some 10,000 acres between Beit Shemesh and Beit Guvrin, not far from Jerusalem. The park is set amid hills about 1100 feet high, with mature natural scrub and planted forests. It is dotted with archeological remains, deep wells, caves, and abandoned fruit gardens. The park is one of many Jewish National Fund nature reserves and was initially funded by donations from Britain.

This is the area where the Philistine giant Goliath was defeated by the youthful David, who later became King of Israel. Before that, it was also the site of one of Israel's most disastrous defeats at the hands of the Philistines, immigrants from the Greek isles with powerful allies around the Mediterranean region. The Philistines had subjugated the Israelites by means of their more advanced iron weapons, made possible by their long held a monopoly on iron-smithing. The biblical description of Goliath's armor is said to be consistent with this iron-smithing technology.

"Now Israel went out to battle against the Philistines, and encamped beside Ebenezer, and the Philistines encamped in Aphek. Then the Philistines put themselves in battle array against

73

Israel. And when they joined battle, Israel was defeated by the Philistines, who killed about four thousand men of the army in the field ... And when the people had come into the camp, the elders of Israel said, 'Why has the Lord defeated us today before the Philistines? Let us bring the Ark of the Covenant of the Lord from Shiloh to us, that when it comes among us it may save us from the hand of our enemies.' So the people sent to Shiloh, that they might bring from there the Ark of the Covenant of the Lord of hosts... And when the Ark of the Covenant of the Lord came into the camp, all Israel shouted so loudly that the earth shook ... So the Philistines were afraid, for they said, 'God has come into the camp!' And they said, 'Woe to us! For such a thing has never happened before. Who will deliver us from the hand of these mighty gods? ... Be strong and conduct yourselves like men, you Philistines that you do not become servants of the Hebrews, as they have been to you. Conduct yourselves like men, and fight!' ... So the Philistines fought, and Israel was defeated, and every man fled to his tent. There was a very great slaughter, and there fell of Israel thirty-thousand foot soldiers. Also the ark of God was captured ..." (I Samuel 4)

Israel was defeated by a combination of superstitious belief in the ark as a talisman (instead of belief in the power of God), their certainty that the Philistines would be overawed by the ark, and the determination of the Philistines to retain their domination of the Israelites. But eventually the Israelites matured and grew stronger than their enemies. The kingdom of David and his son Solomon then became a major power in the region.

We began our hike at the site of a modern Zionist legend, that of the Lamed Hay (the 35). These were the 35 Palmach fighters (precursor to the Israel Defense Forces) who were massacred on their way to aid the beleaguered Etzion bloc of settlements in Judea, following the 1947 UN Partition Plan to divide Palestine between Arabs and Jews. The Jewish villages, bought and first settled by Jews in 1927, fell to the British armed and led Jordan Legion. After a number of Jews were murdered by the Legion, the surviving settlers, both men and women, were taken to Jordan as prisoners of war.

Our route around and through the British Park included a stint on the Cross-Israel trail, which spans the entire length of Israel. Passing through the orchards of the kibbutz Givat Yeshayahu, we began the climb up Tel Azeka to its summit in the park, which afforded us fantastic views in all directions. Tel Azeka is a hill where it is believed the Philistine camp stood when David fought Goliath in the Elah Valley. The Jewish camp was on nearby Mt. Soha. We enjoyed our midmorning snack sitting under almond trees on one of the many monuments situated on the summit.

We continued through the park, noticing the playgrounds for the kids and the parking lots which allow less energetic visitors to reach the summit without an extensive hike. Descending from the highlands to the valley floor, we discovered a culinary adventure there.

Our ultimate destination was the Hans Sternbach Wine Estate, where the main house has become a popular restaurant on weekends. A small winery established in 2000, Sternbach is just one of scores of boutique wineries that now dot Israel. We enjoyed our afternoon supper in the dining room, though several parties were enjoying al fresco dining in the courtyard, which was warmed by the sun to a comfortable temperature. The food was excellent, prepared near to our table in the large home's kitchen. Many of the ingredients were grown right on the premises and everything was prepared to order. We enjoyed washing down our meal with one of the vineyard's red wines, which are made from grapes grown nearby, close to the Elah Valley. Before leaving we had the opportunity to buy delicacies prepared from home-grown produce.

Though our boots had picked up plenty of mud along the way, we all enjoyed the brisk winter weather and great scenery. Hiking in Israel is a popular pastime, both for individuals who journey to the trail by car and for larger groups in buses. It's enjoyed for the exercise and fresh air as well as the historical and archeological highlights. A hike in Israel is something all energetic visitors should try to include in their itinerary, to enjoy a taste of what the locals love to do.

EXPLORING CONTEMPORARY JERUSALEM

In mid-August, we spent the weekend with friends exploring Jerusalem. This time we started with one of Israel's most picturesque venues, the Mahaneh Yehuda Marketplace. For Americans, in particular, this busy outdoor shopping venue is something that can't be duplicated at home or anywhere else.

The name of the marketplace is taken from its neighborhood, which was founded in 1887 by 162 families. During the Ottoman period (until 1917) the growth of the market was haphazard, with sanitation suffering from the frenzied increase in the number of stalls opened for business. Health conditions deteriorated to the point that the British Mandate government stepped in and ordered the closing of the market in the late 1920s.

Fortunately, loans for the merchants were arranged by the Committee of the Jewish Community of Jerusalem, with easy payment terms provided by the Halva'ah ve-Hisahon Bank, whose chairman doubled as the head of the Committee. The bank stipulated that the market be named after itself, and according to the sign still hanging outside the entrance to the market, that's the official name. However, don't expect anyone to know it by anything except Mahaneh Yehuda.

Inside the large marketplace, which is roofed and covers several blocks, a riot of color, aromas, products, and shoppers greets visitors. Since it's Jerusalem, there are always a surprising number of English-speakers wandering through the alleyways, picking up breads, cookies, spices, and all manner of goodies not to be found in their local supermarket. We joined the crowd and bought a hat, baked goods, nuts, and fruit. We thought of stopping at one of the jammed shwarma or falafel stands, but instead opted for lunch at a nearby Kurdish restaurant. There we had kubeh soup, salads, and stuffed vegetables. Delicious!

Afterwards, we wandered around the neighborhood and discovered the square which is the center of the adjacent Even Yisrael neighborhood. Built in 1875, it is the sixth housing development built outside the Old City walls. The Jerusalem municipality has displayed a number of permanent placards in the square, which include pictures of the original settlers and their families, including formal portraits taken at weddings, etc. The wedding picture of one of the neighborhood's prominent families, taken near the end of the 19th century, shows a variety of ethnic types, some of whom look Turkish, some Spanish, some North African, and others European. Similar displays can be found in other Jerusalem neighborhoods.

We spent the night at the Regency Hotel on Mt. Scopus, next to the Hebrew University's main campus. Originally part of the Hyatt chain, the hotel was designed in 1991 by David Resnik, one of Israel's most prominent architects at the time. The hotel's seven cloistered courtyards and multilevel atrium lobby are terraced down the slope of Mt. Scopus, affording great views of the city.

On Shabbat morning, after the usual sumptuous hotel buffet breakfast, we drove to Abu Tor, near the Old City. We started our walking tour just below the beautiful Sherover Promenade and overlooked the Peace Forest below us and the UN (formerly British) Government House on the far side of the valley. Incidentally, fifty years ago, when Israel planted the Peace Forest consisting of 100,000 trees, Jordan asked the Security Council to intervene against Israel's "aggression"!

During the War of Independence, Israel took control of the upper part of the quarter, while Jordan retained the lower part and the cease-fire line bisected the neighborhood. We walked up one of the steep streets of the neighborhood, which was once a "no-man's land" between Israel and Jordan. In several locations we saw "fortresses" (large homes) in which troops from both sides observed a relatively peaceful coexistence. However, shots were occasionally fired and there were several fatalities in the period from 1948 to 1967.

Abu Tor is the Arab name for the neighborhood, but prior to 1967 when the area was divided between Jordan and Israel, the Jewish section was called Hananiah Hill, after a Second Temple period High Priest. "Abu Tor" was the name of a general who served Saladin, the Kurdish Muslim warrior who conquered Jerusalem from the Crusaders. The general was given the hill which bears his name by Saladin as a reward for valor. The neighborhood also has a Christian connection. It is identified as the Hill of Evil Counsel, where the Sanhedrin (an assembly of Jewish judges who constituted the supreme court and legislative body of ancient Israel) supposedly decided to hand over Jesus to Pontius Pilate for judgment.

Since 1967, Abu Tor has been one of the most successfully mixed (Arab-Jewish) neighborhoods in Jerusalem. The original homes have been joined by many modern ones, owned by upper income families. Abu Tor enjoys some of the most dramatic views in the city. As we walked down the far side of the neighborhood, we enjoyed the dramatic vista below - the Old City and the Mount of Olives.

By this time, we were ready for a rest. We stopped at the delightful Mt. Zion Hotel on Hebron Road. This medium-sized hotel is situated in an old (1882) Turkish building, on the plunging slopes of the Valley of Hinnom, facing Mount Zion and the Old City. It is surrounded by biblical and historical sites, but its most charming aspects are its "oriental" furnishings and ambiance. Even the public bathrooms are gorgeous! We enjoyed refreshments in the delightful lobby, seated next to huge arched windows with the most fantastic view. We all resolved to spend our next vacation in Jerusalem at the Mt. Zion.

Before returning to our hotel we checked out the nearby cable car, which was secretly installed during the War of Independence to supply Jewish troops just across the valley on Mt. Zion, behind the Old City walls. The cable was lowered onto the valley floor during the day and only used after dark. Its location remained a military secret which wasn't revealed until after the Six Day War.

We relaxed for the remainder of the afternoon around the Regency Hotel pool. After checking out, we attended the final evening of the Jerusalem International Arts and Crafts fair. Enjoying our choices from the numerous ethnic food stands inside the entrance, we walked around the fair, viewing the interesting artistic offerings and listening to the many musicians. It was a great finish to a terrific weekend in Jerusalem, the city that symbolizes the outstanding combination of history and recreation that is available in Israel.

"PLEASE TOUCH" THEATER AT JAFFA PORT

We recently attended a show at the Nalaga'at Center in the dilapidated Jaffa port, located in the southern quarter of Tel Aviv-Jaffa. Housed in a renovated warehouse, the center is part of the rehabilitation of what was once Palestine's main seaport. The port area is eventually expected to be a big tourist draw, similar to the booming Tel Aviv "Port" in the northern part of the city.

The "Nalaga'at" nonprofit organization opened in December 2007. The Center consists of the "Nalaga'at" Theater, home to the Deaf-blind Acting Ensemble; Café Kapish, with its deaf waiters and BlackOut, the pitch-black restaurant with its staff of blind waiters. The "Nalaga'at" Center currently employs some 70 people, most of whom are deaf, blind or deaf-blind.

At the center, whose name means "Please Touch" in Hebrew, the idea is to turn "normal" life upside down by empowering deaf and blind people while pushing seeing and hearing customers beyond their comfort zone. Although it is billed as the world's first professional deaf-blind theater company, most of the actors are also mute. Touch is the primary mode of communication, though a few of the actors have enough residual vision to read sign language, in Hebrew or Russian.

Adina Tal, founder and director of Nalaga'at Center, says: "These deaf-blind individuals, who, all their life had been dependent on society and assisted, were all of a sudden in an entirely different situation. Standing on the stage, they were no longer 'the poor ones', 'requesting' commiseration, but those who were in the position to 'give', offering their audience the gift of art."

The actors are of various origins, but they were mostly born deaf and then became blind through illness. Brothers Igor and Yuri emigrated from the former Soviet Union (FSU). Igor dreams of watching TV. Yuri is married with two daughters and especially enjoys reading. Another Yuri, Marc and Genia are also emigrants from the FSU. Nurani emigrated from Iran. Rafi and Itzik were born in Israel, as were sisters Zipora and Bat Sheva. Shoshana came to Israel from Romania and dreams of joining others in normal conversation.

"Not by Bread Alone" is being presented this season to sold-out audiences. Eleven deaf-blind actors take the audience on a magical tour in the districts of their inner world; the world of darkness, silence and … bread. As the process of bread making unfolds on stage - the dough is actually being kneaded, raised and baked - a unique encounter occurs between actors and audience. Together they reenact vivid or distant memories, recall forgotten dreams and joyful moments and "touch the divine spark" present in everyone.

The actors take the spectators into those magical moments between reality and fantasy, between grandeur and ridicule, and eventually return to the basic meaning of bread as a symbol of everyone's longing for a home. "[Man lives] Not by Bread Alone" – the actors declare, repeatedly emphasizing the importance of their interaction with the audience and their need for relationships, which is even more crucial than is the need for bread.

While all the actors were accomplished, several stood out. Itzik Hanuna, who can speak, was the master of ceremonies, usually seated off to the side typing on his Braille typewriter. Born blind, he became deaf at age 11 after being ill with meningitis. He writes poetry on his typewriter and is able to recite it in his heartrending voice. His method of "hearing" is for a translator to touch specific finger joints on Itzik's hands, at blazing speed, to spell out what is transpiring.

Bat Sheva Ravenseri, a mother of three, is a beautiful woman with an aristocratic and knowing air. "Before the theatre, I lived a regular deaf-blind life in darkness and silence. I didn't have a future," she said through a translator, who converted questions into sign language by stroking and squeezing her hands. "I want to show that blind and deaf people also have a lot of strength and love to give," said Ravenseri, who wore an elegant purple dress.

Marc Yarosky has two daughters. (All the children mentioned can see and hear.) Blessed with a mischievous smile and sparkling eyes, Marc has a gift for physical comedy. He says that he takes pride in being a real gentleman. His stage presence was such that you wouldn't even know that he is visually impaired.

"Not by Bread Alone" is inspirational, to say the least. I defy anyone to feel sorry for themselves after seeing this show. Despite their disabilities, the actors are very professional and they manage to engender empathy in the audience, who are able to follow the action on stage in Hebrew/English/Arabic subtitles, and Hebrew sign language. Reflecting on the show, I felt that I'd been treated to a complete performance despite the fact that only several of the actors had actually spoken.

Hopefully, Nalaga'at will prove to be a wonderful example to similar groups around the world. On subsequent visits we expect to visit the café, which looked intriguing, and the BlackOut restaurant, which has gained a reputation as an absolutely amazing experience. There are workshops in sign language, pottery and wine tasting – the latter two in total darkness. Not the least of the accomplishments of the Nalaga'at Center is that it attracts a wide audience: Jews, Muslims, and even illegal immigrants from North Africa. You can find out more about this unique facility at: www.nalagaat.org.il

THE JEWISH QUARTER OF JERUSALEM

Going up to Jerusalem during Succot is always an amazing experience. Succot is one of Judaism's three pilgrimage holidays - the other two are Pesach and Shavuot. More than almost any other holiday, these three hearken back to life in the Land of Israel in biblical times. During First and Second Temple times, Jewish pilgrims came to Jerusalem to make thanksgiving offerings to God, ranging from doves to livestock. To get an idea of what Jerusalem was like in those days, I recommend a trip to the Davidson Exhibition and Virtual Reconstruction Center in Jerusalem's Archeological Park, adjacent to the Southern Wall of the Temple Mount.

The Jewish Quarter of the Old City is one of four quarters: Jewish, Armenian, Christian, and Muslim, which are surrounded by the wall constructed by the Muslim ruler Suleiman in the mid 16th century. At the end of Israel's War of Independence, the Jordanians controlled the Old City, including the Jewish Quarter. They devastated the Jewish homes and institutions, going so far as to dismantle synagogues and use their stone blocks as paving stones for urinals. In the Six Day War, Israel regained the entire Old City and began to completely rebuild the Jewish Quarter.

During Succot we went on an AACI (Association of Americans and Canadians in Israel) tour of the Jewish Quarter, conducted by a pert senior citizen. The tour began at the Four Sephardi Synagogues, which are all located in one building. (Sephardi Jews are descendants of Jews who lived in the Iberian Peninsula, and later in North Africa and Asia, after 70 CE.) We descended into the building, which was built slightly below street level to fulfill the Muslim prohibition against synagogues being higher than any mosque nearby.

The first synagogue is dedicated to Yohanan ben Zakkai, whose academy was located on this site before the destruction of the Second Temple. Ben Zakkai became leader of the Sanhedrin (the high council) when it was forced to relocate from Jerusalem to Yavne. Unusually, the synagogue has two Torah arks, for which there are several conflicting explanations. The large, beautiful Sephardi-style synagogue has a striking mural of prophetic visions above the arks, as well as a high niche in a window on the adjacent wall which contains a shofar (ram's horn) and a cruse of oil. These represent remnants from Temple times, kept in place for use by the Messiah when he arrives.

The next room contains the Eliyahu Ha-navi (Elijah the Prophet) Synagogue. Its name comes from this legend: one Yom Kippur, when a tenth man was needed to create a minyan (quorum for prayers), an old man suddenly appeared to complete the minyan and then disappeared after the long day of prayers. The worshipers realized that this stranger was the prophet Elijah. They dedicated an ornate chair to him, a replica of which is in an adjoining alcove. The magnificent, dark wood Torah ark came from Padua, Italy, after WWII.

The middle synagogue, Kahal Zion, built in the former courtyard between the other two is smaller but also contains a succah. The last of the four synagogues is the Istanbuli Synagogue, built by Turkish immigrants but used by all the Sephardic communities. It has both a Torah Ark and a reader's podium from Italy.

We left the Four Synagogues and wandered through the Quarter, which was very crowded with tourists and Israelis coming to the Old City for the holiday. We passed the ruins of the Tiferet Israel Synagogue, whose beautiful facade with four arches still stands. It was founded by Ashkenazi Jews (descendants of Jews from Western and Central Europe, who left Judea after 70 CE) who had originally settled in Hebron. The construction was only finished when Austrian emperor Franz-Josef donated the funds to build the dome, after visiting Jerusalem and seeing his former subjects' synagogue in an incomplete state.

Across the street is the Karaite Synagogue, which is watched over by the last remaining Karaite family in Jerusalem. The Karaites are a sect who split off from rabbinical Judaism in 8th century Baghdad. They accept only the written law, rejecting the oral commentaries of the rabbis. Several obvious differences of the Karaite tradition are in their dietary laws, their kindling of lights (electricity) on Shabbat, and their type of mezuzah, which is a tablet on the doorpost of a house rather than a small container holding an inscribed prayer. More than 20,000 Karaites still live in Israel, out of a global population of about 30,000.

We then entered the Bet Mahase Square, which is large and contains two significant buildings. The first, built in the mid-19th century, consists of one hundred three-room, subsidized apartments to help alleviate the tremendous crowding in the quarter then. Because of the development's clean, paved courtyard and well plastered water cistern, the apartments were highly prized. One-third of the units were allocated to Hungarian Jews, one-third to Dutch Jews, and the remaining third to diverse poor Jews. This square became the last stronghold of the Jews who defended the Jewish Quarter in 1948. The soldiers who were captured there when the war ended were sent to prisoner-of-war camps in Jordan. The large building on the western side of the square was built with a donation from Baron Rothschild of Frankfurt in 1871. Several columns from the Roman period are situated in front of it. Both buildings have been revamped and are used for community and educational purposes today.

From the square we went to an overlook of the Western Wall plaza. As expected, we saw thousands of people congregating and praying under the towering wall of large stone blocks, with more people entering the plaza than exiting. The Western Wall (Kotel) is the remnant of the retaining wall of the platform on which the First and Second Temples stood. On the way to our last destination we passed the Hurvah Synagogue. After the Jordanian capture of the Old City in 1948, all that remained of the destroyed synagogue were scattered stone blocks. In 1967 the victorious Israelis built a symbolic arch to mark the height of the original dome. Recently, funds were raised to restore the synagogue to its former glory. The rebuilt Hurvah Synagogue is a symbol of the resurgent Jewish Quarter, which is home to thousands of observant Jews from all economic sectors.

We finished our tour at the Old Yishuv Courtyard Museum, which is located in a small alley connecting the Jewish and Armenian Quarters. Unlike many of the courtyards in the Jewish Quarter, which were rented to Jews by Arab landlords, this structure was owned by Jews. The Weingarten family, descendants of one of the first Ashkenazi settlers in the quarter, recovered their home after the Six Day War and converted it into a unique museum. Its rooms now contain furniture and implements used by the Ashkenazi and

Sephardi families who once lived in the quarter. There are numerous photographs and histories of the Quarter's inhabitants, including one of the matriarchs who founded the still-existing Berman Baking Company, one hundred and fifty years ago.

Exiting the Old City through the famous Jaffa Gate, we continued directly into the new Mamilla commercial development, built on the seam line that divided Jerusalem from 1948 until 1967. This unique mall combines new construction and buildings dating back centuries. We had supper in the succah of the packed Rimon (Pomegranate) Café, where the throng of people waiting to enter nearly blocked our exit. The custom of making a pilgrimage to Jerusalem during Succot is alive and well in Jerusalem, 3,000 years after its founding as the heart and capital of the Land of Israel.

JERUSALEM FILM FESTIVAL

We recently returned from a four-day vacation in Jerusalem. Michal and I and our friends Shaike and Ros stayed in a rented apartment in the Katamon neighborhood, just minutes from the Jerusalem Cinematheque. We were also close to the Old City, the German Colony, Rehavia, and Talbiyeh, all of which are among the most interesting locales in Jerusalem. The proximity to the Cinematheque was important because we came to town to attend the annual Jerusalem International Film Festival.

This yearly festival of documentaries and feature films from around the world originated in 1984, the brainchild of Lia and Wim van Leer. Lia was the director of the first 24 festivals, only giving up direct control this year, the Festival's 25th anniversary. She and her late husband, a Dutch engineer, pilot, playwright and film producer, opened Israel's first film club in Haifa in 1955, which later became the Haifa Cinematheque. The van Leers opened several other cinematheques in Israel, including this one in Jerusalem in 1981. Lia van Leer was awarded the prestigious Israel Prize for her creative projects in 2002.

I've been attending the Festival for a number of years, but each time for only a day to see a few movies. This year we wanted to get into the spirit of things and see a half-dozen films. We were lucky to find a small apartment for short-term rental in Katamon, one of Jerusalem's most pleasant neighborhoods, having a nice mix of religious and secular families. The name "Katamon" comes from the Greek words for "near the monastery", referring to the nearby San Simon monastery. The Katamon Quarter was developed during the British Mandate period, mostly by Greek

Orthodox Arab entrepreneurs from the Jerusalem area. They intended it to be an upper-class Arab neighborhood, like Rehavia and Talbiyeh were.

About a hundred homes were built in the 1920s and 1930s on land bought from the Greek Orthodox Patriarchate, which is still a major land owner in Jerusalem. The one-floor homes were usually inhabited by their owners. The extra apartments in houses of two or three floors were rented by other Arabs. The neighborhood's original buildings have elaborate masonry work, ornamental metal grills, courtyards, gardens, and stone walls or iron fences around the properties.

In late 1947, just before Israel's War of Independence, various sites in Katamon were used by local Arab irregular forces to attack Jews. Heavier fighting occurred once Israel declared its independence in May 1948. By then the nearby British army base had been evacuated and the British officials and army officers had left their homes in Katamon. After the Jews conquered the quarter in the War of Independence, it was abandoned by its Arab inhabitants. The first new inhabitants were refugees from the Jewish Quarter of the Old City, who had lost their own homes when the Jordanian Arab Legionnaires kicked them out. Later, families of new immigrants moved into Katamon. The neighborhood didn't ever attain the high level of Talbiyeh or Rehavia, but its great location and many nice apartment buildings make it a very desirable neighborhood in its own right. (See "Jerusalem - a walk through time" by Yad ben-Tzvi.)

The evening of our arrival, we saw a Yiddush feature film, "The Jester", about an itinerant Jew who wandered into a small shtetl in

Galicia (now part of Moldova and the Ukraine) and got a job with a cobbler. In the 1937 film, there's a scene where the "jester" plays a leading role in a Purim spiel, upsetting the shtetl's social order. Parts of the Purim spiel were infamously used in a Nazi anti-Semitic propaganda film, "The Eternal Jew".

The next morning we had breakfast with David Rubinger, the famous Israeli photographer, in one of the German Colony's many cafés. David's photographs are among the best known in Israeli iconography, most notably his photo of three paratroopers gazing at the liberated Western Wall during the Six Day War of 1967. (Search on the Internet for David Rubinger and click on "images".) David told us how he had moved to Israel from Vienna as a teenager in 1939 and other adventures. He has lived through tempestuous times in Israel, including the horrific murder of his wife by an Arab gardener, but he retains an optimistic outlook on life and appears far younger than his age. David's latest book, a memoir and personal history of Israel with many of his photographs, is "Israel Through My Lens: Sixty Years As a Photojournalist", which is highly recommended.

We were fortunate in the additional five movies that we picked. Because there are too many to choose from, one's choices are greatly dependent on the scheduling of the films. That day, after our pleasant and informative repast with David, we saw "Acne", a film about a Jewish adolescent in Uruguay suffering from acne and the other usual teenage travails. Later in the day we were somewhat shocked by an interesting documentary from England, "The Lie of the Land". It was about British farm policies which wreak havoc with small farmers there.

The next day our choices emphasized food. First we saw "The Chicken, the Fish, and the King Crab". This documentary covered the Bocuse D'Or, an international food preparation contest founded by legendary French chef, Paul Bocuse. In the evening we saw an excellent feature film from Brazil, "Estomago - A Gastronomic Story". This gritty drama featured a down-and-out guy who learned to cook, a friendly but always-hungry streetwalker, and a restaurateur who took them both under his wing. It had a gruesome but poetic ending. In between the two movies we prepared Shabbat dinner in our apartment, hosting our older son Moshe and his girlfriend on Moshe's 27th birthday.

On the last day of the ten-day festival, Michal and Ros saw a documentary about the Amazon, while Shaike and I were awed by a Korean film, "The Chaser", about a disgraced detective turned pimp who had to chase down a serial killer of call girls.

Our four-day interlude in Jerusalem was terrific. While we are used to frequent trips there for the day or evening, having the chance to live in Jerusalem, if only for several days, made us muse about actually residing there one day. There's no denying it, Jerusalem is one of the most special cities on earth. But don't just take my word for it - any season of the year is a fabulous time to see for yourself.

Encountering Israel – the North

HOLIDAY ON THE GOLAN

We almost missed a great time in the Golan Heights recently, but for a good reason. Our younger son Shaul was coming home for the weekend after his first week in the Paratroop Brigade of the Israel Defense Forces. For most Israeli families, the entry of their children into the IDF is a definite rite of passage — and we're no exception. Shaul had just passed a grueling five-day exercise designed to choose the best of the new entrants. He was very pleased, and we were too. The top priority for the weekend was getting the new recruit filled with home cooking and his clothes washed. After that came much-needed sleep, so early Saturday morning we were free to travel up north, while Shaul slept through most of the day.

Northern Israel is full of "zimmers", inexpensive B&Bs for tourists that are either part of someone's house or an additional purpose-built structure. It's a great way for the owners to make extra income while providing a needed service for vacationers. We were heading to one close to the Lebanese border to meet friends for the day. They had already done some great activities: kayaking on the Hatzbani River, hiking, and a fabulous evening tour of the Nimrod fortress, which dates back to the time of the Crusaders. While touring, they had met a group of American college students on a Birthright trip, which are free, guided tours to Israel arranged for Jewish young adults from around the world.

By 10 a.m., we had eaten a leisurely breakfast with our friends and were on the way to the Banias Spring parking area. We stopped at the Tel Faqr Memorial, which commemorates a fierce battle in the Golan during the Six Day War of 1967. This was made much more memorable for us because one of our companions had fought there that day. Luckily for Shaike, his unit arrived at the battle scene after the firefight. Thirty-one Israelis died in that attack.

Tel Faqr was the Syrian's second line of defense on the northern Golan slope and was relatively unknown to the Israelis, who had quickly overcome the forward Syrian outpost. Shaike told us that the ominous sound of the artillery shells gave a 90-second-warning, which wasn't enough time for many of the embattled soldiers to find cover. Artillery and other fire devastated the Israeli troops, many of whom were caught in their transport vehicles when they burst into flame. Overcoming Tel Faqr was crucial for defeating the Syrians, who turned and ran back towards Damascus when their attempts to stop the Israeli defense failed.

We started our hike near the Banias Spring, along the Banias River, past the wonderful Banias Falls. The name "Banias" comes from the Greek god, Pan, which was pronounced "ban" in Arabic. We were able to stop and dip our feet and our steamy heads into the river, after we had left the crowds near the falls behind. We ended our hike midway between the source of the Banias and its convergence with the Hatzbani and Dan rivers. Our stopping point gave us a gorgeous view of the mountains abutting the Golan Heights.

After a refreshing swim back at the zimmer, we had dinner at the restaurant of Kibbutz Goshrim, where our table was nestled literally on the banks of the Dan River, almost in the water. We ate fresh fish from the river and enjoyed our recollections of the day, particularly the panorama of Israeli communities and the Hula Valley far below.

Capsule history: The Golan Heights, an area of about 460 square miles, contains the remains of many ancient Jewish settlements. It was included in the Palestine Mandate that Britain was given by the League of Nations in 1923, to establish a homeland for the Jews in Palestine. Just a few weeks later, the colonial powers Britain and France traded territories to better preserve their influence in the Middle East. The result was that the Golan Heights became part of French colonial territory and was included in the state of Syrian founded in 1946, while Britain gained control of Iraq. From 1946 to 1967, Syria took advantage of its position in the Golan overlooking Israel's Hula Valley to shell Jewish settlements below and to launch military incursions. Israel won full possession of the Golan Heights during the Six Day War in 1967; it was put under full Israeli law in 1981 by then Prime Minister Menachem Begin. Its Druze villagers remain, still citizens of Syria, but now residents of Israel. There are about 20,000 Druze on the Golan living alongside an equal number of Israelis.

JOURNEY TO AKKO

We recently joined other eager touring enthusiasts on a bus to Akko, the modern name for the ancient city of Acre, once one of the strongest and richest city-states on the eastern Mediterranean. In the distant past, the powerful Hasmonean king Alexander Yannai, descended from the Maccabees, failed to conquer Akko. Napoleon also failed to do so. Before the War of Independence in 1948 several Jewish patriots were hanged there by the British, but a few days later the Jews brilliantly blew a hole in the ancient walls and all the remaining Jewish prisoners escaped (along with many Arab ones). Most recently, Akko was named a UNESCO World Heritage site, which has been the impetus for an influx of development funds and renewed interest in this walled city.

Dating back some 4,000 years, Akko was originally a fishing village which developed into a bustling port city, with a diverse population including Jews, Christians, and pagans. In the 7th century the Arabs invaded, replacing the Jewish and Christian religious sites with Muslim ones. In the 12th century, the Crusaders invaded Palestine to depose the "infidels" (Jews and Muslims). They made Akko their effective capital, although nominally Jerusalem had that honor. Many of the outstanding sites in the city date back to the Crusaders and to the triumphant Arabs who eventually overthrew them, after two hundred more years of warfare.

The most attractive sites in the old city of Akko include ancient Hellenistic and Roman remnants, the "underground" Crusader city, Ottoman quarters, and the El-Jazzar mosque - built on the remains of a Crusader monastery - one of the most important

Muslim sites in Israel. The Crusader quarters were abandoned and later covered by dirt and debris up to 30 feet. For example, we saw pictures of the hole in the wall through which Jewish forces attacked the Crusader fort, which the British used as a prison. In the pictures, the hole is just above ground level. Yet we saw it from a courtyard about three stories below! The excavations of the Crusader city by the Old Acre Development Company began in the 1950s and continue today, as the city of Akko improves the sites to encourage tourists. We saw vaulted halls where Crusaders lived and a section of the tunnel which led outside of the city, built by the Templars (military/monastic) Order.

The governor of Akko, known as El-Jazzar, was an omnipotent pasha (governor) for the Ottoman rulers. He was known as a cruel man - he carried an axe which he used to behead or otherwise mutilate his subjects, often on a whim. It is said that he slew all 37 of his harem when he was unable to identify by sight the one who betrayed him with another man. We saw a painting of El-Jazzar and his entourage, one of whom had only one eye. In addition to the axe, El-Jazzar also used a poker with which he poked out the eye(s) of those who offended him. In this case, the unlucky advisor was a court Jew, who was later rehabilitated and continued to serve El-Jazzar, only to be killed eventually by the next pasha. Regardless of his brutality, it was El-Jazzar who revitalized the city, which had fallen back into a small fishing village following the defeat of the Crusaders.

Jazzar Pasha built the city walls which prevented its takeover by Napoleon's army in 1799. Napoleon, fresh from victories in El-Arish, Jaffa, and Haifa, overestimated his army's capabilities when it came to Akko. At that time, the British were also active in

Palestine. Admiral Sidney Smith sunk the French fleet and captured Napoleon's heavy artillery, forcing Napoleon to rely on his depleted ground troops, which numbered in the thousands. While they were successful in punching a hole in the city's formidable wall and laying siege to the city for sixty days, the French were constantly harassed by El-Jazzar's troops. Napoleon was hard-pressed to defend himself against both Arab and British fighters. Ultimately, Napoleon retreated with his men, who were disheartened and ravaged by disease.

An outstanding reconstructed site from El-Jazzar's era is the Al Baha Hammam (Turkish bath). The baths were a social center for rest and entertainment, where the wealthy could hold banquets for their friends. They were a meeting place for both the prominent and the common people. There is an entertaining and educational sound/light/virtual reality presentation which led us through the rooms of the renovated baths, which have exquisite tiles and beautiful domed ceilings with natural sunlight filtering through small, circular glass openings.

Before leaving Akko, we visited the Baha'i gardens outside the Old City. The founder of the religion, Baha'ullah, was sent to Akko from Persia by Ottoman authorities. He died in Akko in 1892 and was buried there, which is why Israel is the world center of the Baha'i faith. Baha'ullah's burial place, the Baha'i shrine, is surrounded by beautiful gardens. These gardens are built horizontally in a formal style. While not as incredible as the vertical Baha'i Gardens in Haifa, they are nevertheless well worth seeing.

Our only regret was that we didn't have enough time to dine at one of Akko's famous port-side restaurants. But since we know that the archeological digging is continuing nonstop there, we're looking forward to returning before too long to have a fine dinner after seeing some new discoveries.

CARMEL NATIONAL PARK

With fellow members of ESRA, we drove in private cars to the Carmel National Park on Israel's northern coast. Mt. Carmel, with its wild cliffs and green landscapes, is a symbol of beauty close to Israel's urban areas. Its special characteristics have also made it a part of religious tradition. On Mt. Carmel Elijah performed one of his best-known miracles. He called on God to send fire from heaven to consume the pagan sacrifices which had been placed on the altar by the priests of Baal. Following this convincing demonstration of the difference between God and idolatry, the priests were put to death on Elijah's orders and the Israelites were convinced to turn back to the one, true God (see 1 Kings 18).

Jews, Druze, Muslims and Christians sanctify Mt. Carmel's sites, the Carmelite order of Catholic monks bears its name, and Mt. Carmel is also the location of The Shrine of the Báb, the holiest site of the Baha'i faith.

Mt. Carmel is 16 miles long by 4-5 miles wide and 1,800 feet high. The city of Haifa is situated at the western promontory of Mount Carmel and partly at its base, close to smaller Israeli and Druze towns. The park covers 21,000 acres, one-third of which are nature reserves. The national park is entirely dedicated to the protection of Mediterranean nature and landscape and features forest and woodland species of trees, as well as shrubs, numerous flowers and a variety of wildlife, along with wonderful panoramas and archeological sites going back to the dawn of humanity. From 1930 to 1932, at Mt. Carmel, Dorothy Garrod excavated Neanderthal and early modern human remains in the "Carmel Caves", producing a record spanning 600,000 or more years of human activity. (See www.parks.org.il and http://eraexcellent.co.il for more information.)

Starting from the parking lot adjacent to the artists' village of Ein Hod, we rapidly climbed the mountain and soon reached a dramatic scenic overlook. Since Mt. Carmel is located along the Mediterranean seashore, we were treated to a fabulous panorama overlooking the sea. We glimpsed the ruins of the Crusader fort at Atlit; the barracks where the Jewish "illegal immigrants" were imprisoned by the British, during the years when terrorized Jews fled the Nazis trying to enter Palestine; and the site of the agricultural research station built by Aaron Aaronsohn. He was the famous Romanian-born Jewish agronomist, botanist, traveler, entrepreneur, and Zionist politician who took up residence in Palestine when it was still a Turkish province. Aaronsohn, who was killed in a plane crash in 1919, is known as the discoverer of wild emmer, which he believed to be "the mother of wheat." He was also the founder and head of Nili, a ring of Jewish residents of Palestine who spied for Britain during World War I.

We continued our slow ascent of the mountain and shortly found ourselves walking alongside of limestone cliffs. Due to the extreme porosity of limestone, there are many caves on the mountain. We entered one of them and were surprised at its size. Since it was pitch black, we used flashlights to illuminate the way. At the cave's terminus, our guide Almog told us to extinguish the lights. We then noticed a source of light coming from a narrow "chimney", which was only observable from one particular spot.

While walking we saw some of the first winter flowers of the season, in white, pink and yellow hues. We came to a WWII fortified outlook overlooking the sea, in which lookouts were placed to discover Nazi infiltrators coming into Palestine from the sea. Fortifications like this proved unnecessary, however, when the German army was stopped in North Africa.

We then had a steep quarter mile climb to a plateau below the top of the mountain, where our trail became more level. During most of our hike we alternated between sun and shade, and since the temperature was in the low 70s, the conditions were ideal. Almog pointed out a geographical oddity, a vertical "pipe" in the sheer limestone wall next to the trail. Caused by erosion, this pipe is a feature of the cliffs in the area. We ate our lunch at a sunny spot adjacent to a ruined stone domicile, which caused us to wonder who had lived in this isolated spot and when it was built.

Our route through the park is a segment of Israel's longest hiking trail, the Israel National Trail, a footpath that winds its way from the Red Sea in the south to the Syrian/Lebanese border in the north. The trail crosses the Negev Desert, past three seas (actually, large lakes), alongside ancient ruins and through modern cities. About 600 miles long, the trail can be traversed in as short a time as 30 days, but most hikers prefer to do one small stretch at a time, as we were doing. Others hike for several days, either camping on the trail or staying at a nearby B&B, hostel, or kibbutz hotel.

On our last leg of the hike, we left the Israel Trail and walked on a level stretch frequented by families and school groups. We followed a stream which originated from a mountain spring, along which were orchards of various fruits, palm trees, and some ancient ruins.

Carmel National Park is one of Israel's most popular and accessible parks. We were lucky to have hiked there on so perfect a fall day, relatively unhindered by the many casual hikers who park close to the most popular attractions in the park. We could have finished this excellent - and at times strenuous - hike with a visit to Ein Hod's artist studios, cafés and galleries, but that will wait for another day.

TO THE HULA VALLEY

Linda, my friend and part-time editor, recently accompanied her two granddaughters and their father, Ilan, on a trip to the fabulous Hula Valley in the northern Galilee. I've included her commentary below. They spent the evening before their adventure in the Galilee panhandle town of Kiryat Shmona, which is close to the Lebanese border. The town, sitting on the western slopes of the Hula Valley, is named in honor of eight of Israel's pioneering heroes and was built as a "development town". These are communities originally meant to disperse Israel's population away from its crowded center as well as to house new immigrants.

After the 1948 War of Independence, Kiryat Shmona was founded as a transit camp for immigrants, mostly of Sephardi descent, who worked in agricultural projects in the area. Today a town of about 20,000 residents, Kiryat Shmona's pleasant spring and summer weather attracts many tourists and Israelis on holiday. Besides the many B&Bs in the area, the nearby kibbutzim of Hagoshrim, Kefar Giladi, and Kefar Blum all provide hotel accommodations and many tourist activities.

Visiting the Hula Valley is a popular choice for Israelis of all sorts and birdwatchers from around the world – but its history is particularly interesting to anyone. Hula Lake is one of the oldest documented lakes in history: under the name "Samchuna", it was mentioned in the Tel el Amarna letters of Pharaoh Amenhothep IV in the 14th Century BCE. The name "Hula" is related to a Second Temple Period locality called in Aramaic, Hulata or Ulata. This name survived in Arabic as "Buheirat el Hule", which is similar to its modern Hebrew translation.

Before the lake was drained, the Hula Valley comprised a lake at the southern end and swamps in the north. The swamp consisted, for the most part, of an impenetrable tangle of papyrus, interspersed with channels of running water and pools. Up to 70% of the Jewish pioneers in the area suffered terribly from malaria emanating from the Hula swampland. (www.migal-life.co.il)

Several years after the declaration of the State of Israel in 1948, the government began to drain the swamps and the lake, covering more than 15 thousand acres at the time, to convert them into agricultural fields. The project became the standard bearer of the entire Zionist movement: the resettling of the land and the re-establishment of the Jewish National Home in Israel. Nevertheless, scientists and nature lovers waged a vigorous battle to conserve at least part of the original landscape. In 1954, the government agreed to set aside 800 acres of the pond for Israel's first nature reserve. Two hundred and fifty acres of wasteland just north of the Hula Nature Reserve were re-flooded forty years later, when environmental considerations became prominent, bringing the park to its present size. (www.parks.org.il)

Linda described to me the spectacular sunrise over the Golan Heights visible from Kiryat Shmona, as the beautiful valley below became swathed in glorious morning light. She continued: "Since no Israeli day can begin without 'breakfast', we enjoyed ours at one of the many picnic tables on the grounds inside the Hula Valley Nature Reserve. Once the families we were traveling with had agreed as to which vehicle we'd hire to take us around the 7 mile trail, we were off in two vehicles, best described as golf carts - one joined to the other - with Ilan at the helm - and six joyous little girls shouting "Yeah, yeah, yeah."

The grandfather of our group was an elderly 'Crocodile Dundee' type, replete with hat and long red hair who had an excellent knowledge of birds and creatures, their names (in both Hebrew and English), and their habits. One father in the group, a professional photographer, also knew a lot about the fauna of the area and had a camera with amazing lenses. I'd say all the adults were there because they wanted to impart their love of nature to their daughters and granddaughters.

And what nature we are blessed with! Along the banks of the fairly deep canals which run along the rim of the irregular-shaped medium-sized lake, we saw dozens of baby turtles resting on muddy land ... each one plopping into the water as we stopped to look at them. A water badger also obliged us by keeping dry for a while in the sun. Fields of wheat, planted not long before, were on one side, while on the other was the huge (for Israel) lake, albeit much smaller today than the original lake and swampland of the '50s. We stopped whenever a special bird or creature came into view, got out to take a closer look and then continued on our way. Also on these roads were a few other visitors, some walking, some on bicycles, others on special tricycles or golf carts. We were lucky enough to have missed the heavy traffic but we did see a tractor pulling an open coach full of religious woman on our return to the visitors' center.

We parked alongside the beautiful lake with its lush vegetation. There, one of the rangers had his enormous zoom lens focused on some of what must have been about five million birds, each type in its designated area in the shallow lake and on little man-made islands in the middle of the lake - islands which provide protected nesting sites for some of the species. There were massive flocks of migratory storks (apparently 100,000 of them fly past and stop in this valley, with a quarter of them not moving on), cormorants, cranes, and other birds standing in the water or standing on land – more than 200 species in all. Blanks are fired sporadically in order to minimize the damage from the flocks of birds to the agriculture in the nearby fields, causing the birds to fly off. What a sight to see them up in the air like arrows as they fly in formation! There are also colonies of herons, kingfishers, kites and other species, which the more learned among us were happy to point out. We all managed to keep quiet from time to time in this noiseless atmosphere, where only the incessant singing and chattering of the birds filled the air.

Our next long stop was a circular observatory on a slightly raised piece of ground. Each window in the observatory provided a new and exciting outlook onto the lake and the canals, with ducks paddling through the water forming a V-shape in their wake. All around us were lush vegetation and flocks of birds ... enough to dazzle the eye. Also grazing on the green fields we saw water buffalo on one side and swamp horses and donkeys on the other. As far as the eye could see, it was a picturesque and dream-like scene of tranquility against the backdrop of the Golan Heights. No human habitation, other than a kibbutz nestled on its lower slopes, was visible.

It was lunch time when we returned to the visitors' center, (but not before we'd stopped next to the largest pelican I've ever seen, who posed for us so gracefully) so out came the food again, filling empty and not-so-empty stomachs. Goodbyes were said and on we moved homewards.

On our return journey, as the sun was nearly setting and the clouds were turning pink, several flocks of birds flew above us in amazing formations, a scene which had even my younger granddaughter amazed at the wonder of it all. A special ending to a superb day which exceeded even my expectations!" Thanks to Linda for her beautiful description of what was certainly a great experience for the entire group.

THE ESSENCE OF ISRAEL – THE GOLAN HEIGHTS

The month of Tishrei is one of the busiest in the Jewish calendar. The High Holidays, Succot and Simchat Torah are all celebrated during this month. In addition, Tishrei always comes at one of the most pleasant times in Israel, when summer wanes and the first rains of the season clear the air. We recently combined this period of holiday prayers and feasts with an exciting hike in the north of the country.

It's impossible to give those of you who haven't experienced the High Holidays in Israel the real flavor of what it's like, but once you've been here during this season, it's unforgettable. For a week before Rosh Hashanah the anticipation of the holiday runs high and everyone is greeted with wishes for a "good year". Then, before Yom Kippur, the greeting is for a "good signature/listing in the Book of Life". Of course, the all-purpose "happy holiday" is heard throughout the month from everyone.

While the day of Rosh Hashanah is not radically different in Israel from what it is in the Diaspora (except for simple white clothing instead of being all-dressed-up), there is nowhere like Israel for Yom Kippur. That's because no one drives on the holiday and the only moving vehicles are bicycles. We attend services in one of the seven congregations that are available in our town, Alfe Menashe. Besides the two permanent synagogues, one Ashkenazi and one Sephardic, there are three other Sephardi groups, one Yemenite, and one Hassidic.

I would be misleading you if I didn't mention the fact that a great number of Israelis literally flee the country at this time, figuring that the many days off from work and school are a perfect time for a family vacation. While I think these very secular Israelis really miss out, it's their choice. Many other secular Israelis refrain from going to synagogue but still enjoy the all-encompassing atmosphere. As for me, the absolute stillness of a whole day (actually 25 hours) magnifies immeasurably the benefits of the Day of Atonement. Finding three stars in the night sky on the way home after services finish, and then breaking the fast in our ancient homeland, concludes an incomparable day.

On the weekend between Rosh Hashanah and Yom Kippur we traveled north to the Golan Heights with the ESRA hiking club to the Banias Nature Reserve. The Hermon stream originates from Mt. Hermon, the highest peak in the region. These springs create the Banias, Dan, and Hazbani streams, which together form the headwaters of the famed Jordan River. We started our hike at the Banias Springs, adjacent to the remains of the Greek Temple of Pan, the Greek god associated with nature. The entire area was later controlled by the Romans, who attached it to the kingdom of Herod the Great at the end of the first century BCE. There Herod built the luxurious temple to Pan – said to be the most opulent of its type constructed in such a natural setting.

We hiked past beautiful vistas and a strongly flowing stream by the hydroelectric station which provided electricity for the Syrian village of Banias until 1967. We then entered the middle level of the three-floor Matroof flour mill, which has been partially reconstructed to show the workings of the water-powered mill, including a view of the large mill stones at the bottom (water) level. Villagers from miles around once brought their wheat to this mill. Continuing on, we reached an "officers' pool", one of many concrete pools built on top of springs used by the Syrian army when they controlled the Golan Heights before the Six Day War. We passed the point where the disused Iraq-Lebanon oil pipeline is located, buried beneath the stream bed. Next, we came to another flour mill, this time entering on the top level. After pausing at the waterfall lookout, we reached the Banias Waterfall itself, which was still impressive even at the end of the dry season.

Leaving the fenced-in reserve, we stopped for lunch at a unique mosaic-decorated kiosk, whose grounds are "air-conditioned" by water misters located above the gated entrances. After lunch, we changed into bathing suits and went back to the Banias stream, this time to hike through it. Because of the lack of rain the water level was relatively low, assuring us of tough going since many rocks protruded above the water. (During the rainy winter and into spring the Banias is better described as a river, which can accommodate rafts and canoes.) We hesitantly felt our way through the sometimes-swift current, resorting to floating on our backs when the stream was too wild to negotiate on foot. The water walk was an exhilarating concluding segment, even better in retrospect: We did it! It was a long day, but our group returned to the center of the country pleased with the exercise, fresh air, and companionship.

A week later, we assembled and decorated our succah in preparation for the holiday of Succot. For us, the essence of life in Israel is that holidays come and go, the seasons change, and we live in land promised to us by God. Our Jewish heritage is all around us, waiting to be discovered. How things turn out depends on our efforts, but also on the whim of God, fate, luck, or however you like to describe it.

RETURN TO THE NORTH – NAHARIYA

After the ceasefire ending the Second Lebanese War in 2006, we were anxious to travel north to the Galilee region. Our purpose was twofold. First, Israelis love to spend time in one of the most scenic regions in the country. Second, we wanted to support the population there and spend money in the tourist attractions, which had taken such a beating during the month-plus hostilities.

We took an inland route to our first destination to avoid Haifa's clogged roadways and arrived in Nahariya in just an hour and a half. Nahariya is a pleasant coastal town near the Lebanese border, known for its main street with a canal running along it. We checked into the Carlton Hotel on the main drag, a few blocks from the beach. When the hotel was built decades ago the view was unbroken to the sea. Now the view is obscured, but since the hotel was recently renovated we found it quite enjoyable.

We soon left the seashore with our friends and headed inland towards the Montfort Castle, a popular archeological attraction. Located in the Western Galilee, the fortress rises 600 feet above the Kziv River, which is one of the only rivers in the area which flows year-round. Montfort can be seen from across the gorge by tourists; for those who enjoy hiking, there are long and short routes towards the castle. Due to our late start, we chose the shorter hike.

Montfort Castle was built by the Knights Templars in the mid-12th century. One of three Crusader orders formed to cleanse the Holy Land of the infidels (Muslims and Jews), the Templars built Montfort as a feudal agricultural development. But in 1187 the castle was conquered by the great general, Saladin, after his rout of the Crusaders at the nearby Horns of Hattin. Within a short time the Crusaders retook the fort and soon sold it to the Teutonic Knights, who changed its name from Montfort (strong mountain) to Starkenberg, which has the same meaning in German.

Because the fortress is accessible only from one side, it remained impregnable until near the end of the 13th th century, when a long siege by the Mamluk ruler Beibars succeeded in forcing the Crusaders to surrender. However, the Muslim victors were so impressed by the fortitude of their adversaries that they allowed the Crusaders to retreat from Montfort with their valuable historical archive, which can be seen today in the Austrian Tyrol. We especially enjoyed the shade of the fortress remnants and the beautiful views of the Galilee forests and the Mediterranean Sea in the distance. (See www.gemsinisrael.com for more details on this and other worthwhile places.)

Returning to Nahariya, we stopped for lunch at a branch of one of the many coffee "restocafé" chains in Israel, which have usurped the place of the former dairy café chains which dominated the restaurant scene for decades.

After an afternoon by the pool, we sauntered down to the beach along the main promenade, whose canal is empty until the winter rains replenish the Galilee streams and rivers which feed into it. The promenade was crowded with young people on vacation as well as families with kids in tow. The many cafés and restaurants are crowded together alongside the familiar tourist shops which can be seen in beach resorts everywhere. At the beachfront there are many other places to unwind, but these feature alcohol rather than coffee and food. We stopped at a pleasant venue which offered some of everything and had a simple but delicious supper on the outside deck. One couple had to return home that evening, so they left early to catch the train to Herzliya from the station, conveniently located at the beginning of the promenade.

In the morning, after the usual sumptuous Israeli hotel breakfast, we walked around town. Nahariya was initially settled by German Jews fleeing the Nazi regime in the 1930s. Its history is told at the Lieberman House, which is now the city museum. In 1934, the pioneers of Nahariya bought two large plots of land from the Tuwaini family, absentee landlords from Lebanon. The Lieberman House is typical of the ones built by Jewish immigrants from Germany, known as "Yekkes". The Lieberman family built a thriving agricultural business in the area and their children continued in agricultural endeavors or became professionals.

During the Arab pogroms of the late 1930s, the British Mandate police (composed of Jews and Arabs) protected the growing town, while other communal agricultural settlements were built in the area. Beginning in 1942, the Lieberman House was a base of operations for the Palmach (Haganah resistance group's armed wing) under the command of Yitzhak Rabin, later an Israeli prime minister. Illegal immigrants often spent their first night in the Yishuv at the Lieberman House, which became the site of a recuperation center for the injured after the War of Independence.

Another interesting site in Nahariya is the Water Tower. It was one of the first structures built in town and the well beneath it provided the town's water for more than fifty years. There is a hidden basement in which soldiers were trained to fight during the Arab disturbances of the 1930s. Later, one of the tower's floors became a guards' station and the tower's rooftop was used for transmitting Morse code signals via heliograph (a movable mirror that reflects beams of light) up and down the coast. The roof was also an observation post for spotting enemy ships and planes during WWII. Now the water tower is a cultural and historical center.

On our way home we stopped at the nearby Beit Lohamei Haghetaot kibbutz, the Ghetto Fighters kibbutz. It was established after WWII by Holocaust survivors, including some who had fought the Germans as ghetto fighters and partisans. The kibbutz is home to an outstanding Holocaust museum, with special emphasis on Jewish resistance movements. The museum is a valuable resource for refuting claims that all Jews went to their slaughter like lambs. We learned that there were at least nine instances of organized resistance to the Nazis by Jewish captives, including three major ones.

The largest and best known resistance event was the Warsaw Ghetto Uprising of April 1943, which the museum treats in great detail. After examining the historical documents and artifacts displayed in the museum, visitors leave with a much better understanding of what it was like to confront the organized evil that the Nazi regime perpetrated on the Jews. Besides visitors like us, the museum hosts large groups of students and young soldiers. After such a busy weekend, we were glad to head for home, only a short trip if one avoids the crowded coastal highway - which we did.

GALILEE WEEKEND - SAFED

We recently headed north with our friends to the scenic Galilee region to celebrate Michal's special birthday. We were on our way to Safed in the Upper Galilee, but we had enough time for a diversion on the way.

A perfect place to visit was the Kadoorie Agricultural School at the foot of Mt. Tavor, founded in 1933 by Sir Ellis Kadoorie. The Kadoorie clan lived and prospered in Baghdad for thousands of years before a branch of the family migrated eastward to Bombay (Mumbai) in India. They flourished there and in the mid-19th century some of the family moved to Shanghai, and later Hong Kong, to extend their business interests. Now counted among the wealthiest families in the world, the Kadoorie family is renowned for its philanthropy.

We began our tour of the beautiful and expansive Kadoorie village with the Agricultural Farm and the Research Center. The manager of the farm graciously took the time to show us around the cow and sheep sheds where we learned that Israel is the most advanced dairy producer in the world. For example, the yield from dairy cows in Israel is unmatched anywhere. Another factoid: Israel has the largest variety of white cheeses (sour cream, cottage cheese, etc.)

There are 1400 students in grades 7-12 at the village school, which has three divisions: junior high, high school, and a junior college specializing in engineering. The 9th graders are required to live in the village, while it's optional for other students. It's the 9th graders who take responsibility for the care of the animals, the buildings and the grounds, supervised by professionals. The dairy products of the farm are bought by the huge Tnuva dairy, while meat and other byproducts are also sold. This income helps defray the costs of the educational institutions. From the very beginning, Kadoorie School has given emphasis to agricultural studies. The farm includes animal husbandry (cows, sheep and horses) and plant life (field cultivation, orchards, and hothouses).

After visiting the farm and the corral, we toured the original barn and police station, now the venue for a fascinating film about the complex. The school has a diverse population, consisting of new immigrants from Ethiopia and the former Soviet Union, together with ethnic minorities from Israel, such as Circassians, Druze, Beduins, and Christian and Moslem Arabs. Many prominent Israeli leaders have been students at Kadoorie School, including Yitzhak Rabin, former general and prime minister of Israel.

The school's motto is, "Living in a multicultural society." Unique educational and social programs have been developed on the subject of multiculturalism including trips, parties and performances for the whole student body. (www.kadoorie.galil.k12.il)

Leaving the beautiful campus, which is not far from the Sea of Galilee (called Lake Kinneret here), we headed to our destination for the long weekend, the Canaan Spa. Located at the top of the city of Safed, which at 2,800 feet is Israel's highest city, the hotel has a commanding view of the town and the surrounding countryside. On clear days the towering Mt. Hermon is easily visible.

Safed is first mentioned in the Talmud (the collection of ancient Rabbinic writings consisting of the Mishnah and the Gemara, constituting the basis of religious authority in Orthodox Judaism), which indicates that it was probably not settled until the time when Rome ruled over Palestine. The town became an important Jewish center in the late 15th and early 16th centuries CE, after Jews began migrating there from Spain, following the start of the Inquisition in 1492. Before that, the town was first dominated by the Crusaders in the late 12th century, who were themselves routed by the Muslims led by Saladin. A half century later the Crusaders re-conquered the town and built a huge fortress, only to be invaded in 1266 by the Mamelukes under Sultan Beibars of Egypt and Syria. Beibars cut off the heads of the men and sold the women and children into slavery. The Mameluke dynasty ruled until 1517, when it was overthrown by the Ottoman Turks, who controlled the entire region for the next four hundred years.

Home to many religious Jews, Safed is one of Judaism's four holy cities. (The others are Jerusalem, Tiberias, and Hebron.) It gained that honor from its association with mysticism and the great rabbis who flocked there. Safed is known as the center of study of the Kabbalah, a very complicated and esoteric Jewish philosophy. Lately, Kabbalah has become popular on a simplistic level with both Jews and non-Jews. Previously, Kabbalah was not recommended for study except by married Jewish men of advanced learning. Famous rabbis like Joseph Caro and Issac Luria lived in Safed. Even today, visitors can visit and pray in tiny synagogues associated with both of these giants.
(www.jewishvirtuallibrary.org)

"At the start of the 17th century, there were 21 synagogues and 18 Jewish schools in the town. Toward the end of the 17th century, the Jewish population declined dramatically, so that by 1764, there were only 50 Sephardic families left. However, a more stable government during the latter part of the 18th century led to the return of many Jews and substantial Eastern European immigration. By 1895, Jews constituted a majority of the population. The population significantly declined after World War I (caused by the 1929 Arab riots throughout Israel, most significantly in Hebron), and at the start of the War of Independence in 1948 the Jewish population was 2,000 out of a total population of 12,000. By the mid-1990s, the population was in excess of 21,000, all Jewish." (www.edwardvictor.com/Safed)

When we visited the Biriya Forest, not far from the Canaan Spa, we found out what happened in 1948 to save Safed for the Jews. The settlement of Biriya was founded outside of Safed in January 1945 on Jewish National Fund prepared land. "Biriya was one of three outpost Galilee settlements, referred to as 'castles', established by the Bnei Akiva [religious] division of the Palmah and Haganah army corps. The soldier-settlers, who built the Biriya stone fortress which includes a tower and walled courtyard, were employed by JNF in forestry work, digging tree wells and planting saplings."

"In February 1946, the British discovered in the fortress an arms 'cache' belonging to the Palmach; they seized the fortress, captured 32 members of the Palmach and sentenced them to the Akko prison on charges of illegal arms possession. Some weeks later, on the 11th of Adar, [commemorating the anniversary of the Tel Hai settlement's founding] 3,000 people, loaded with equipment and personal possessions, established Biriya Bet [the 'second' Biriya]. This operation was nicknamed 'The One-Armed Operation' after Joseph Trumpeldor." [Trumpeldor was the famed

Jewish fighter who had lost an arm fighting for the Russian Army in the Russo-Japanese War, after which he made aliyah. When Trumpeldor was cut down battling the Arabs at Tel Hai, he famously cried out, 'Never mind, it is good to die for our country.']"

"The startled British authorities waited until the crowd had dispersed, set fire to the new settlement, demolished its buildings and imprisoned its defenders. When the news broke, hundreds of people from all over Eretz Israel rushed to Biriya to start rebuilding the destroyed site for the third time. Faced with such Jewish determination, the British Army retreated, allowing the settlers to remain. After Israel's War of Independence, a new immigrants' moshav was established at Biriya." (www.kkl.org.il) It was the fervent, courageous fighters at Biriya – Jews determined to keep the holy city of Safed in Jewish hands – who routed the Arabs and enabled Safed to become part of Israel.

After visiting the Biriya fortress, we continued hiking through the forest, which was resplendent with almond trees and flowers in full bloom. Along the way we noticed empty areas cleared for young saplings. Soon, we came upon a new memorial commemorating gifts which had been received to reforest the areas damaged by Hezbollah missiles in the Second Lebanon War. We spotted some plaques without inscriptions, waiting for additional JNF donors.

The 5,000 acre Biriya forest is mostly planted with Jerusalem pine and is at an elevation of 3,000 feet. There are also other species of pines as well as Atlantic cedars, with typical vegetation and seasonal flowers. There are many paved paths throughout the forest facilitating access to the numerous picnic tables for visitors in wheelchairs. Biriya is also known as the site of many tombs of famous rabbis. We visited the tomb of the son of Yehuda HaNasi (Judah the Prince), who was the editor of the Mishnah in its final form. Many pilgrims come to Safed to visit the tombs, especially on certain holidays.

The city of Safed is undergoing extensive renovations. Long known as an artists' colony, it had become dilapidated in recent decades. During this visit we saw many improvements in the town's infrastructure. Numerous parts of the Old City have been rehabilitated, while construction is in progress in other sections. Tourists were everywhere, frequenting the cafés, studios, galleries, and artisan's shops. We visited an artist, a native of Detroit, whose artwork is based on his Kabbala studies. We saw similar religious motifs in many galleries, reminding us of the great popularity Safed has for both religious and secular visitors.

Besides the miles of walks and trails in the surrounding forests and the tourist-friendly Old City, we really enjoyed the Canaan Spa hotel. Spa facilities in Israel have become increasingly popular, in venues like the Dead Sea and Eilat, as well as day spas in cities and small towns. The Canaan Spa had all the facilities we wanted, including a large indoor pool, a Turkish hamam (an opulent steam room), exercise room, treatment rooms, tea corner, and more. The cuisine was excellent, in the usual Israeli Mediterranean-Middle Eastern style. Whether you live here or come as a tourist, life in Israel is jam-packed with things to do and great places to see!

TOWERS AND COLUMNS - BET SHE'AN

In early winter, Israel's weather is ideal for hiking and touring. With our friend Barry, who was visiting Israel for the second time, we traveled to the Bet She'an Valley, where we stopped initially at Tel Amal (also known as Nir David) and then continued on to Bet She'an National Park.

Jews had been pioneering settlements throughout Palestine for many decades by the time the Nazis came to power in Germany in 1933. The robust German decrees against Jews caused increased Jewish immigration to Palestine. The Arabs, seeing the large influx of Jews from Europe, began a new period of riots in protest, building on the previous, widespread violence in 1929. During April 1936, Jews were attacked in Jaffa, beginning three years of rioting against Jewish settlers. Armed gangs attacked Jews and the British mandatory forces in an attempt to discourage Jewish development efforts. The attackers, under the leadership of the Mufti of Jerusalem Haj Amin el-Husseini, soon extended the rioting to Samaria and Galilee, targeting the most vulnerable and isolated Jewish settlements.

The leaders of the Yishuv decided to expand Jewish settlement efforts by building on Jewish-owned property and on newly purchased land. The crucial elements of this strategy were: to establish settlements on high ground to gain command over the terrain; locate them close to each other; and to have short lines of transport and communication between settlements. December 10, 1936 was the day the first "Tower and Stockade" settlement was built. This achievement was the prototype for 57 similar settlements that were established from 1936 to 1939.

The historic Tel Amal settlement in the Bet She'an Valley was the first to be built. Prefabricated structures, a tower and wooden planks for fencing were secretly transported to the site and erected overnight with the help of volunteers from nearby settlements. The plan included a double layer wooden defense walls about six feet high, several huts for quarters and utility purposes, and a watch tower to serve as a lookout post and for communication. The size of each settlement was set at approximately 110 feet by 110 feet.

Though a special unit of defenders was assigned to each settlement during its setup, some stockades came under attack almost immediately. Five settlers at Tel Amal died while working the nearby fields or during the frequent raids. Despite the continuous Arab attacks and the hardships, none of the 57 settlements was ever abandoned. Everyone traveling to Israel should visit Tel Amar. It is the perfect example of the grit and determination of the early Zionists to settle the Land of Israel against all odds, and helps one to understand the Israeli ethos.

Before we left the totally rebuilt and refurbished tower and stockade at Tel Amar, we were able to wear "period" clothes and try out some of the implements used at the settlements. We also had fun in the adjacent "bell park," which contains makeshift bells, some of which were very loud, that were used in many of the settlements. There is also a small but excellent museum, featuring exhibits covering the Copper Age to the Bronze Age.

We then drove to the nearby Bet She'an National Park, which covers more than 400 acres. Modern excavations began there in the 1920s and in 1986 a major project was begun by the Israel

Antiquities Authority and Hebrew University. So far, about one tenth of the city's area has been uncovered.

Settlements on the site began more than 7,000 years ago. In the 16th century BCE the city was the center of Egyptian rule over the area. By the time of Israel's first king, Saul, the Philistines were the dominant force in the region. Saul and his three sons were killed in a major battle waged at nearby Mt. Gilboa and the Philistine lords of Bet She'an hung their bodies on the city walls (1 Samuel 31:10).

King David, Saul's successor, conquered Bet She'an and the towns of Megiddo and Ta'anach and his son, King Solomon, made Bet She'an his regional capital. Long after the split of Solomon's kingdom, the city was destroyed during the conquest of the Northern Kingdom (Israel) by the Assyrian king, Tiglat-Pilesser III, in 732 BCE. After Alexander the Great's death, during the Hellenistic period, the city was known as Nysa-Scythopolis and its Jewish residents became part of a large cosmopolitan mix.

The Hasmonean dynasty, founded by the Maccabees, conquered the city at the end of the 2nd century BCE, exiling its gentile residents and making the city predominantly Jewish again. This situation lasted until the (first) Roman conquest of 63 BCE, when the Jews were displaced. For the Romans, Bet She'an, then known as Scythopolis, was the most important city in northern Israel. During Roman rule, pagans, Jews and Samaritans lived in the thriving and expanded city, surrounded by magnificent public buildings, statues, and beautiful streets. As the pagan beliefs of the Romans gave way to Christianity, Bet She'an became a mostly Christian Byzantine city, with a population of nearly 40,000. A wall was built around the city and churches and monasteries were located nearby.

After the Arab conquest of the mid-7th century, its importance dwindled along with its loss of inhabitants. Following the severe earthquake of 749 CE, Scythopolis became a minor rural settlement known as Beisan. In the Medieval period, when Crusaders ruled the area, a small fortress was the settlement's major building. The area remained a backwater under the rule of the Ottoman Turks, from 1517 until 1917.

Among the features of the Bet She'an ruins are its hundreds of standing columns, its magnificent streets, the remains of its important buildings, the mosaic floors, and the amphitheater which is still in use. The most dramatic (but hard to photograph) sight of all is the great breadth of the town as you enter the park along its ancient thoroughfares. The most interesting ruins are those of the sophisticated bathhouses and public toilets, which illustrate the high level of civilization attained by the Roman Empire.

We climbed to the top of the Bet She'an tell (20 layers of former civilizations forming a man-made hill, where each level pertains to a distinct period) at the northern edge of the ruins, where are located Stone Age and Egyptian remnants. The view of the ruined city is magnificent but it is equaled by the view of the Galilee in the opposite direction. While there are many ruins in Israel, those at Bet She'an are surpassed only by the ones at Caesarea. Bet She'an is a destination that should not be missed by archeology buffs. (www.jewishvirtuallibrary.org)

GOD'S COUNTRY – THE GALILEE

God said to Moses, "Go up into this mountain of Abarim, and see the land which I have given to the children of Israel." (Numbers 27:12) We did just that recently on the first hike of the 2007-2008 ESRA hiking season. We headed north to Abirim (or Abarim) in the Galilee to begin our hike.

The Galilee is one of Israel's most scenic areas, with elevations averaging between 1,500-2,300 feet. The region encompasses the northern region of Israel, divided into three sections: Upper, Lower, and Western. Both the Upper and Western Galilee are blessed by (relatively) plentiful rainfall, which means we were hiking in verdant areas full of trees and other flora. The fauna in the region is also abundant. The Hula Valley, for example, attracts scores of thousands of migratory birds each year on their way to and from Africa. Our trail, located about twelve miles from the Mediterranean Sea, included exploring the Abirim fortress, walking alongside of, or in, the K'ziv River (which is more like a stream in America), and then ascending from the K'ziv Canyon.

As our bus entered the town of Tarshiha, we saw a crowd of people attending Israel's largest annual Christian-Arab convocation. Tarshiha is half of a unique municipality, which was established by joining the Jewish settlement of Ma'alot with the Arabic settlement of Tarshiha (pronounced Tarshikha). After the security officers OK'd our entrance onto the road leading to the trail, the bus made its way beyond the exhibition grounds up to the parking area near Abirim. We couldn't help but reflect on the irony of the situation: while Israel has been vilified as an apartheid state, a huge Christian gathering was being held here.

Clambering up the rough boulders into the Abirim fortress, we were surprised by its small size. Although this information isn't available on the Internet yet, Gilad, our excellent guide, informed us that the so-called Crusader fortress was probably a family tomb from the Roman-Byzantine era, according to the latest research done under the auspices of the University of Rochester. While the so-called fortress was given that designation due to its proximity to other fortresses, like nearby Montfort Castle, its design, size, and even closer proximity to similar mausoleums contributed to the recent archeological explanation.

We continued into the K'ziv River Canyon. The 15-mile-long canyon, one of Israel's most beautiful, is one of the few river beds with flowing water throughout the year. The river's source is in the Meron mountains. From there it flows into the nearby Mediterranean Sea. The deep canyon that contained the river had hard limestone walls covered with Mediterranean vegetation. We continued past the Mekorot (Israel) Water Company's pumping station on a path which allows easy access to the area for the disabled. Five-sixths of the river's water is used for the needs of the Western Galilee settlements, allowing only the meager balance to flow freely through the canyon, which has been declared a nature reserve.

In certain spots, small wooden bridges cross the shallow river. We had the option to walk along the trail or in the water - most of us took the more adventurous water route. While carefully making my way along the river bed, I was very aware of the uncertainty of each step. Despite my caution, I managed to take a few tumbles, which a few days later continued to remind me of my audacious choice.

Leaving the river behind, we began the long climb from the canyon. While the first part of our hike had been sheltered from the sun, this section was more open. We exchanged the delightful coolness of the water and woods for bright sunshine and heat - but we were amply rewarded for our efforts. As we neared the top of the canyon, impressive vistas opened up in all directions. We eventually made our way to the heights and were then able to enjoy an easy walk, shaded by the many trees.

After a while we came upon an amazing copse of what are called Love trees. These sinuous trees, with smooth, deep red bark, gained their name from a legendary Arab love triangle involving a father, his son, and a beautiful girl. The legend equated the trees with both love and death (blood). In any event, these specimens were the most beautiful we had ever come across, with unique branches, twisted like a unicorns' horns, running parallel to the ground. After admiring the trees, I separated myself from the group to enjoy the solitude of the woods. Striding through the forest on a perfect end-of-summer day was extremely enjoyable, relaxing, and gratifying.

Soon after, as the woods fell behind, we came into the open. On several sides there were mountain views, including Mt. Meron, Israel's second highest peak. On another side, the Mediterranean Sea glistened in the sunlight. It was the perfect ending to another great day-trip with the ESRA hiking group.

GAMLA – MASADA OF THE NORTH

The ESRA hiking group recently took an invigorating and thought-provoking trip to the Golan Heights. The mid-April temperature was not too hot and not too cold, the rain that had been forecast failed to materialize, and the strong winds only buffeted us intermittently. It was a great hike!

On the bus ride north, we enjoyed the lush greenery and rolling hills, soon to turn amber as the heat of summer sets in. The Golan Heights is also extremely beautiful at this time of year. The high plateau, which overlooks the Hula Valley and Lake Kinneret, was full of wildflowers: yellow, blue, purple, white, and even a few red ones, remnants of late winter. The Golan too was very green, the result of the about-average winter rainfall.

Our destination for this hike was Gamla, sometimes known as the Masada of the North. The Talmud (biblical commentary) describes Gamla as a walled city dating from the time of Joshua, at the very beginning of the Israelites' conquest of Canaan, which coincided with the early Bronze Age. The city was abandoned for a time, but was rebuilt in the Hellenistic period (mid-2nd century BCE).

The story of Gamla is perhaps best known through the writing of Flavius Josephus, originally named Joseph, son of Matthias. A very controversial figure in Jewish history, Josephus was born about 37 CE and was a Jerusalem aristocrat. Eager to learn philosophy and the ways of the world, Josephus immersed himself in studies, but also enjoyed adventure. In the year 64, he went to Rome and negotiated the release of Jewish hostages. But when he returned home, Josephus found his country about to challenge the

Roman Empire, whose obnoxious governor Florus had inflamed the Jews against Rome by his confiscatory taxation schemes.

Josephus became a revolutionary and helped to rout the Romans in Jerusalem. He was sent to the Galilee district in the north to organize the populace to fight the Roman legions commanded by Vespasian. General Josephus then supervised the building of the fortifications in Gamla. After failing to protect the prosperous town of Sepphoris (the contemporary Zippori), he and the other defenders decided to draw lots and kill themselves rather than surrender to Vespasian. Somehow, Josephus was the only survivor. After he was captured by the Romans, he quickly ingratiated himself with Vespasian and his son Titus, by predicting that Vespasian would become the Roman emperor. When this eventually happened, Josephus' future was made. To shorten a long story, the turncoat Jewish general was made a Roman citizen, given the name Flavius Josephus, and became a historian whose books are still read today. The gallant Jewish fighter had betrayed his people, but he lived on to write books which chronicle Jewish history in a somewhat sympathetic light.

To return to the subject of Gamla, our group hiked over hills and alongside beautiful ravines to enter the national reserve surrounding Gamla. As we surveyed the precipice shaped like a camel (gamal in Hebrew) far below us on which Gamla was built, we observed that the town was impregnable on three sides, since it was only easily accessible from eastwards. Our guide explained how the town withstood the first Roman siege for seven months, but under the second assault by three Roman legions, led by Vespasian, its walls were breached. Nevertheless, the Romans suffered a humiliating defeat since many of their soldiers were killed. Some time later, after many of Gamla's defenders had slipped away to their homes, Vespasian's son Titus led 200 Romans in a guerilla attack which surprised and overpowered the remaining defenders. In the end, all the inhabitants of Gamla died. The term "Masada of the North" comes from the fact that many of the nine thousand Jewish casualties jumped or were pushed off the utmost heights of the town to their deaths. Josephus chronicled all this in his famous history, "The Jewish War."

As we sat in the impressive ruins of one of the most ancient synagogues of Israel, one which predates the destruction of the Second Temple, our excellent guide, Ilan, led a discussion about the fate of the residents of Gamla. Ilan disputed the idea that the deaths at Gamla were similar to the Jewish Zealots' suicides at Masada. Here, archeological evidence has been found of a furious battle in the town, with serious damage to the synagogue. In addition, the topography of the town lends itself to the theory that the defenders fled to the highest point as their numbers ebbed, only to be killed or thrown off the heights into the ravine.

In any event, Ilan posed the question: who were the greater heroes, those who committed suicide at Masada (where even today some new army recruits have their swearing-in ceremony) or the citizens of Sepphoris, who opened the city's gates to Vespasian's soldiers. Within one hundred years of accepting Roman rule, Sepphoris became the foremost center of Jewish religious and spiritual life in the Land of Israel. The Sanhedrin, the supreme Jewish religious and judicial body, was located there and the prosperous city remained a center of Bible study for centuries. After their destruction, neither Masada nor Gamla were ever rebuilt, in contrast to Sepphoris, which is still vital.

After the arduous 700 foot climb back to the cliffs overlooking Gamla, we walked to the scenic lookout to enjoy some of the most spectacular bird-watching in Israel. Besides the ancient city of Gamla, the park is famous for the large numbers of vultures, eagles, and hawks which frequent this area. While we watched scavenging Griffon vultures gliding between the peaks, a park ranger explained a lot about the avian life in the area. The most interesting fact that we learned about vultures was that they can spot carcasses and other vultures at distances of up to five miles, guaranteeing that any carcass will be the scene of a mass feast. Vultures can consume a huge percentage of their bodyweight in a day, but can also go for a few weeks without eating, if necessary.

Unfortunately, there was not enough time to walk to the nearby Gamla Waterfall and the birds' nesting cliffs before the park closed, but we were able to enjoy the Dolmen trail which leads to the waterfall. Dolmens are small structures made of two large upright stones and a flat capstone, which date back about 5,000 years and were probably used for funereal rites. The monuments provided an interesting conclusion to our unforgettable trip to the Golan Heights and the Gamla Nature Reserve.

See www.livius.org, www.netours.com, and other sites for more on Josephus Flavius and the Jewish Revolt.

A DAY IN HAIFA

It was a beautiful morning in late December when we set off on the coastal highway towards Haifa, just an hour or so northwest of Alfe Menashe. Along the way, we noticed new construction on the beach front. Developers are building up most of the available land along the Mediterranean coast, resulting in high-rises galore. This growth is a product of Israel's fertility rate - the developed world's highest - and the increase in home sales to wealthy Jewish North Americans and Europeans who want a "safe haven" and vacation place in Israel. There is also an increase in the number of Christian Zionists who love to spend extended periods here.

Further north we passed Jisr az-Zarqa, an Israeli-Arab village, the only wholly Arab town on the Mediterranean coastline in Israel. During and after the War of Independence, other Arabs living on the coast fled or were forced from their seaside towns. Notwithstanding that, the cities of Akko, Haifa, Tel-Aviv-Jaffa, Lod, and others, all have large Arab populations.

Located just north of the wealthy town of Caesarea, Jisr az-Zarqa has been problematic since its beginnings in the 19th century. It was founded by black Sudanese, probably brought to the area by Napoleon to serve his troops. From the beginning, the villagers were shunned by the other Arabs in the area. Working for the residents of Caesarea has proven to be the most lucrative means of employment for the townspeople, but relations between the two communities are not good. A barrier separating the towns, built by Caesarea to distance itself from the noise of loudspeakers at the mosques and gunfire from revelers at celebrations, hasn't helped matters. Though it is relatively dilapidated, Jisr az-Zarqa has a fine beach and a modern sports/social center provided by the government, similar to the ones in nearly every Israeli town.

Entering Haifa, we quickly found a parking space at the foot of Ben-Gurion Boulevard in the German Colony. From this vantage point, the view upwards towards the Carmel Mountain features the glorious Baha'i Gardens ... but more about that later. The German Templer neighborhood was established in 1868. The Templers purchased land outside of Haifa, which then had only 4,000 residents. They also established other colonies in Jerusalem, Tel Aviv, Haifa, and throughout Palestine.

The Templers took their name from the German Temple Society, which strictly followed the New Testament. They intended to build the first planned agricultural community in the Holy Land. Today, they are mostly known for the large, beautiful stone homes they constructed. The Templers prospered in Palestine but suffered as a result of their German affiliations during the two World Wars, when members of the community sided with the Germans. In 1947, the Templers were deported from Palestine to Australia by the British. Eventually, in 1962, they were compensated for their lost properties by the Israeli government.

We continued walking towards Wadi Nisnas, Haifa's only Arab neighborhood that has preserved its original character. It typifies the religious and communal coexistence of Haifa, with its stone houses, narrow alleyways, and oriental-style market. Because of its picturesque buildings and streets, Wadi Nisnas hosts the annual three faiths festival, the Festival of Festivals, held during the Christmas season. On the way there, we couldn't resist stopping at Mama Pita's, a hole-in-the-wall shop with people crowding the entrance. We sampled the cheap and tasty pita pizza, topped with salty cheese and za'atar (hyssop). Delicious!

We had a hard time sticking together in the midst of the festival crowds, but we enjoyed an antiques exhibition, musical events, hawkers selling everything you can imagine, crowded pastry shops with mouthwatering displays, and a felafel restaurant with a loud greeter ("The best felafel in Israel!" he proclaimed) giving out free samples to entice customers to buy. There was a street art competition in the area, so we looked at the walls, roofs ... even dustbins for their particular artistic messages. After we grew tired of fighting the crowds, we walked leisurely out of Wadi Nisnas to the lower terrace of the Baha'i Gardens.

The Baha'i Faith, a post-Islamic monotheistic religion, was founded in mid 19th century Persia and has about six million adherents today, spread throughout the world. More than two million live in India, with the balance residing in nearly all the world's countries. Israel is the center of the Baha'i Faith and hosts its most prominent sites: the terraced Baha'i Gardens of Haifa, including the tomb of the messianic Baha'i precursor "the Bab", and the mausoleum of the founder Baha'u'llah, which is in Akko. Since its inception, the Baha'i religion has faced persecution from some Islamic authorities, because it defies the Islamic teaching that Mohammed is the last prophet.

The gardens themselves are magnificent, with terraces cascading from the upper city down the Carmel slopes to the foot of Ben-Gurion Boulevard, which ends near the water. Everything growing in the gardens is pristine and beautifully maintained by the devotees of the faith, who volunteer to spend time at the shrine.

Almost unbelievably, the beautiful lawns, shrubs, and trees are maintained without man-made irrigation. It's a "must see" attraction in Israel, which explains why reservations are needed to tour the gardens, which is accomplished by descending the many sets of stairs from top to bottom. Even without entering the grandiose gates, tourists like us were able to enjoy the view and the ambiance near the bottom entrance.

Tired by now, we rested on upholstered chairs and sofas, listening to good music in the lovely garden of an attractive coffee bar/ restaurant. We were just biding our time until our reservation time at the Isabella Restaurant, located in a Templer building on the boulevard. We enjoyed excellent Italian-style scaloppini there, the only place we've found in Israel that serves it. On our way out, we were thankful that we had made reservations, since there was quite a throng of hungry people waiting at the entrance. So ended a lovely day in Haifa, port city and industrial capital of Israel's north.

CAESAREA - THE LONG VIEW

Many people know that Caesarea (or Caesaria) was an ancient Jewish port, built by King Herod, which rivaled the best harbors in the eastern Mediterranean. It's also known for its Roman ruins and Crusader fortress. But our recent trip there really illuminated the entire history of this great archeological site, which attracts thousands of Israelis and tourists, especially on a pleasant day like the one when we visited.

Located next to the modern town of Caesarea, an upscale, year-round community with a golf course, fabulous villas, holiday apartments, and a nearby modern industrial area, ancient Caesarea has a long history. Though King Herod is generally thought to have founded the city, he constructed it at the site of Straton's Tower (350 BCE), which originally may have been a colony of Sidon, a great Phoenician commercial empire located on the Mediterranean coast of Lebanon, dating back at least to 4,000 BCE. Straton's Tower is thought to have been named after a Sidonian king in the 4th century BCE, or alternatively, a Ptolemaic general in the 3rd century BCE. (After Alexander the Great's death, the Ptolemy dynasty in Egypt was founded by one of his generals. Another general founded the Eastern Seleucid dynasty.)

A Hasmonean king, Alexander Jannaeus (or Yannai), conquered the town in 103 BCE. Later, the Romans awarded it to Herod and it was he who constructed Caesarea and its harbor Sebastos in 22-10 BCE to honor the Roman Augustus Caesar, who had made Herod puppet king over the Jews. Herod, whose mother was a Nabatean, had been appointed by his father, Antipater the

Idumaean, to be governor of the Galilee region. Most Idumaeans had been forced to convert to Judaism, but they were never totally accepted as Jews because of their continued affection for Hellenistic, pagan values. To cement his position as a leader of the Jews, Herod banished his wife and son and married Mariamne. She was the daughter of Hyrcanus II, the last Jewish king of Hasmonean lineage.

Herod the Great was a monster. Many historians of antiquity hypothesize that he suffered throughout his lifetime from depression and paranoia. Herod murdered 45 members of the Sanhedrin (Jewish leadership) as well as many family members and numerous others. Not only that, he was married ten times! The suffix "the Great" which is attached to his name is appropriate because he was both a great tyrant and a great builder. Herod constructed several palaces, including the one at Masada. His renovation of the Second Temple in Jerusalem was a masterpiece known throughout the ancient world. But even the Temple was dwarfed by Caesarea, a magnificent city and harbor, completed in just twelve years!

During its brief heyday, which lasted only about a generation, Caesarea became the most prosperous port city in the region, and probably the largest city in Judea, with a population exceeding 100,000. Sebastos was as large as Piræus, Athen's harbor. Caesarea was a planned city with a network of streets, a huge Temple to Zeus, a theater, amphitheater, markets, and living quarters. Its water was transported from about five miles away by a Roman aqueduct. Naturally, Caesarea became a great commercial center, populated by Jews, gentiles, and Roman soldiers.

The port itself, the largest artificial harbor yet built, was a marvel of engineering. It utilized hydraulic concrete composed of volcanic ash from Mt. Vesuvius placed in large wooden containers, which became concretized when immersed in the sea. The resulting concrete blocks formed the foundation of the harbor, which was partially surrounded by a wide breakwater with warehouses and docks. Despite its magnificent construction, the harbor was all but destroyed by storms within a few score years of its completion.

Another upheaval for the city was the rift between the gentile majority and the Jews, which triggered the outbreak of the disastrous (for the Jews) Great Jewish Revolt in 66 CE. Nevertheless, Caesarea remained a prosperous city of Christians, pagans, Jews, and Samaritans. By the 3rd century it had become the center of Byzantine Christianity in Palestine (Palestina, the name given to the province by the Romans after the sack of Jerusalem), with the largest ecclesiastical library of the time. A perimeter wall was built by the end of the 6th century, making Caesarea the largest fortified city in the region. But the wall didn't protect the city from the Muslim conquest, which swept through Palestine in the year 638, just sixteen years after Mohammed's rise to power. Under Muslim rule the city became a small, forsaken village, stripped of its political and economic significance.

Baldwin, a noble from France, was one of the leaders of the First Crusade in 1096, which was partially successful. In 1101, Baldwin was crowned King of Jerusalem by the Orthodox Patriarch. During that year, Baldwin liberated Caesarea from Muslim rule, with assistance from a Genoese fleet. The Crusaders rebuilt the city and refortified it. After having languished for several hundred years, Caesarea recovered somewhat as trade around the Mediterranean surged. It remained a stronghold of Orthodox Christianity until Saladin conquered most of the Kingdom of Jerusalem, which included Caesarea, following the Battle of Hattin in 1187.

In response to Saladin's triumphs, King Richard I of England (the Lionheart) led the Third Crusade to recover the Holy Land. But in 1192, the disappointed king returned home. His meager accomplishments were permission from Saladin to allow Christian pilgrims to enter Jerusalem and a remaining sliver of the Crusader (Latin) Kingdom along the Mediterranean which included Caesarea. In 1265, the Muslim general Beibars led the Mamluke army (former slave-soldiers who had evolved into a powerful caste) north from Egypt to conquer Caesarea and the rest of the Christian holdings. After seizing Caesarea and its silted-in harbor, Beibars razed its fortifications, as he did in all the defeated Crusader cities. For many centuries, the ruins of the destroyed and deserted site were used only as a source of lime and building stones.

It wasn't until the late 19th century that the ruling (Muslim) Ottoman Turks began to resettle the city, building new houses on the ruins for Bosnian refugees. (The Bosnian fishermen prospered for a while, but by the time of Israel's War of Independence, they had dwindled and the village was conquered by Israel.) In 1873, the Palestine Exploration Fund began exploring the site. Archeological finds were discovered and removed, as was the custom then. Extensive excavations were begun in 1959 by Israeli and Italian teams. Caesarea became a national park in the 1960s and much work has continued under Israeli and American guidance.

We and another couple were able to sample some of Caesarea's many attractions during this visit, such as the palace, the amphitheater, the Temple platform, the fortified city, the hippodrome, the Roman and Byzantine walls, and the harbor. Not only that, we also took advantage of the new "Caesarea Experience", which included a short but fascinating film and computer generated "interviews" with notables from Caesarea's past and we ascended the "Time Tower" to view a huge three-dimensional animated display, which put everything into perspective, historically and geographically.

We were disappointed, after our tour, that several of the seaside restaurants had long lines with two-hour waits, but the wonderful meal we enjoyed at a slightly more expensive dining spot capped off our wonderful visit to Caesarea, where you're guaranteed to see something newly uncovered on every visit. (www.jewishvirtuallibrary.org)

MODERN CAESAREA

I've already written about the ancient city of Caesarea, its archeological park, its antiquities and its fabulous port several times ... now I'm describing modern Caesarea, a vital city with beautiful neighborhoods, a new high-tech industrial area, and even Israel's sole 18-hole golf course. Recently, Michal and I joined her summer hiking buddies for a birthday outing spent meandering through modern Caesarea and the Ralli Museum.

It was significant for the establishment of Israel that, in 1882, Baron Edmond Benjamin James de Rothschild (1845 – 1934) became an ardent Zionist and began buying land in Palestine. As a leading proponent of the Zionist movement, he provided the land for the pioneering agricultural colony at Rishon LeZion and other places. Rothschild promoted industrialization and economic development, buying more than 125,000 acres of land to set up business ventures.

In 1948, the Rothschild family, through the Caesarea Edmond Benjamin de Rothschild Foundation, purchased the land which makes up modern Caesarea - land which was vacant and disused when the War of Independence ended. Although all the other Rothschild land was turned over to the State of Israel, in 1952 the Caesarea portion was leased back for 200 years by a new charitable foundation, known as the Caesarea Development Corporation (CDC), which has responsibility for maintaining Caesarea. The CDC transfers all profits from the development of Caesarea to the Foundation (half owned by the State of Israel), which supports organizations that advance higher education and culture across Israel.

The great grandson of the Baron continues to head the CDC, making Caesarea the only locality in Israel managed by a private organization rather than a municipal government. CDC provides all the locality's municipal services, markets land for development, manages the nearby industrial park, and runs Caesarea's golf course and country club. The result, and the Baron's legacy, is a unique community that combines quality of life, green concerns, industry, and tourism.

As we began our walk through some of Caesarea's exclusive neighborhoods, we noticed the medallions in the sidewalks designating the CDC management; much more noticeable were the line of fish statues situated on the grass near the sidewalk. These large statues were all imaginatively decorated by the local school children, with mosaics, found objects, and in other creative ways. We soon arrived at a park which contained the ruins of the Palace of the Bird Mosaic, a 45 ft. by 50 ft.floor of a mansion dating from the Byzantine Period, about 1,300 years ago. Actually, there was almost nothing left of what must have been a huge structure, but the mosaic floor of the main salon was remarkably well-preserved, with intricate, geometric patterns of various fish and other animals around the perimeter.

Our walk continued past many "villas" (the term used here for freestanding single family homes), most of them large, some of them beautiful, and all of them very expensive. As we stared at the geometric-shaped, marble roof (!) on one low-slung villa, the owner, who was lounging by the pool, invited in our group of eight to see the garden. He explained that the house was shaped like an airplane and the direction it was facing was towards Jerusalem. Only in Israel!

After a walk of a few hours, we arrived at the Ralli Museum, opposite the town center. The large, private museum was built by Harry Recanati. His family's fortune came from the ownership and sale of the Overseas Shipping Group, IDB Holdings, and the family's Swiss bank - Discount Bank and Trust. The family is among Israel's richest. But it's not that simple ...

Harry Recanati was born in Salonica, Greece, in 1919, to Leon Recanati and Matilde Saporta. The Recanati family was of Italian origin, the Saporta of Sephardi origin, both well known, honorable families. After finishing his studies, Harry joined the modest Palestine Discount Bank Ltd. in Tel Aviv (the name "Palestine" was replaced by "Israel" in 1948), which had been founded by his father just two years previously. The bank was unique in that it was open to private customers, unlike the other few dozen banks operating in Palestine then, which catered mostly to business people and companies. By the end of 1952, under Harry's management, the bank's name had been changed to IDB. It had become the second largest bank in Israel and Harry's younger brother Daniel had joined his brother in running the business. The third brother, Raphael, went into the shipping business, after deciding that banking was a "parasitical" activity.

During 1952, Harry moved the bank's base to Geneva and created a network of affiliated banks in Switzerland, France, Uruguay, Peru and Chile. Ten years later, IDB and a partner bought the Ralli Brothers Ltd., an old established London bank with extensive non-banking interests throughout the world, prompting Harry to relocate to London. Dissension grew between the three brothers when Raphael left the shipping business and established the New

York branch of the Israel Discount Bank Ltd. in 1969. Harry decided to withdraw from the partnership.

What irked Harry the most was his brothers' insistence on taking the bank public. This nullified Leon Recanati's cardinal principle that his bank should always remain under Sephardi ownership, to provide banking facilities to the Sephardi community, where none had existed previously. Harry was aghast that his father's dream of a first-class, private, Sephardi bank in Israel was about to unravel and he refused to participate in taking the bank public.

Harry soon bought two modest banks from his brothers, one in Switzerland and one in France. After successfully running the banks for ten years, he sold out and retired to devote himself to other activities: music, history, and especially, art.

Notwithstanding the somewhat sensationalistic family history (there's a prominent wall plaque dissociating Harry from other Recanatis), the Ralli Museum is quite magnificent. So far, five Ralli Museums have been established in various countries and admission to all of them is free of charge. The original building (Museum 1) in Caesarea holds Harry's huge collection of mostly surrealistic Latin American art, plus a number of works by the Spaniard, Salvador Dali. The second, newer building contains European art from the 16th to 18th centuries illustrating biblical themes. What is unusual about the artwork on display is that although it is all of high quality, many of the artists are relatively unknown outside of their native countries.

To me, the most exceptional feature of the two buildings was that Museum 2 is very reminiscent of the Alhambra Palace in Granada, Spain. The courtyard even includes a replica of Alhambra's

Fountain of the Lions. Near the fountain are several statues of prominent Sephardic Jews from the Middle Ages, including some persons said to be of Jewish descent, such as Christopher Columbus. Lining the walls of the courtyard are many plaques explaining aspects of Sephardi Judaism in Spain during the so-called Golden Age - the period of approximately two centuries preceding the Expulsion of the Jews from Spain in 1492.

After our wanderings through the two Ralli Museums, we went off to celebrate the birthdays of two in our group. A leisurely lunch and two birthday cakes later, we congratulated ourselves on a terrific day spent in modern Caesarea, a town which would have remained a ruin, if not for the foresight of Baron Edmond Benjamin James de Rothschild.

IN MT. TAVOR'S SHADOW

Our recent hike near Mt. Tavor (or Tabor), sponsored by ESRA, was fantastic! The description of the hike promised a steep descent and then a walk along the Tavor Stream (Nahal Tavor) through oceans of flowers, then via the basalt canyon to a strenuous ascent ending in Kibbutz Gazit, where we were promised a wonderful view. We'd done this walk several years ago with friends and we remembered the frequent crisscrossing of the stream and the incredible display of flowers. This time we learned a lot more of the area's history from our excellent guide, Gilad.

The oldest reference to this area is from the time of the Egyptian pharaoh Thutmose III, who ruled from 1,479-1,425 BCE. When his father died, the heir was too young to assume the throne, so Hatshepsut, the royal (first) wife of Thutmose II became regent of Egypt, then coregent with her stepson. Hatshepsut was unique for being the only female pharaoh, and a very successful one at that. She reigned for 22 years until her death (all pharaohs had life terms). Thutmose III, who'd served his stepmother as military chief, then became Pharaoh until his own death, 32 years later.

Thutmose III was a military genius who greatly expanded the Egyptian Empire, from the land of Punt in eastern Africa (today's Ethiopia) to north of the Euphrates River (today's Syria and Iraq). We were hiking near where Thutmose fought a major battle during the first of his seventeen military expeditions. This was the Battle of Megiddo in 1457 BCE. Thutmose outsmarted his opponent, the King of Kadesh, by maneuvering his warriors through a narrow mountain pass, thereby taking the Canaanite forces by surprise. The defeated king was forced to flee with his surviving soldiers to

Megiddo, where they eventually succumbed to a lengthy Egyptian siege.

Thutmose's victory gave him control of upper Canaan. Further north, the Syrian princes were obligated to send tribute to Thutmose, and so were the Assyrian, Babylonian, and Hittite kings. Thutmose had his deeds inscribed on the walls of Egypt's chief temple at Karnak. So it was that the Battle of Megiddo became the first conflict to be recorded in detail for posterity.

Megiddo is doubly significant in the region's history. The second Battle of Megiddo was fought and won during WWI by the British general, Edmund Allenby, against the Turks. It became Britain's most significant victory in its conquest of Palestine. Allenby valued his victory so highly that when he was made a peer, he took the title First Viscount Allenby of Megiddo. I would be remiss if I didn't mention the future Battle of Armageddon, which the Book of Revelation (New Testament) places at Megiddo, where the armies of God and Satan are said to fight their ultimate battle.

Our hike began with a steep trail which took us hundreds of feet down into the canyon. Once there, we began walking through the woods and meadows alongside of the Tavor Stream. During the late winter in Israel, serious hikers, families, scouts, and school groups converge on the most flower-laden areas. This day was no exception, but, luckily, we had the way mostly to ourselves until late in the afternoon. We soon came upon a glorious sight, vast red fields of anemones. Further along, we were engulfed by equally large blue fields of lupines. The expanses of red and blue must be seen to be appreciated. We also passed spectacular fields where we found many varieties of flowers blanketed together in all their beauty and colors, which included red, blue, pink, yellow, and white.

A few of the hikers, anticipating the wet conditions that we would come across, wore water shoes or rubber sandals. The rest of us tried to pick our way carefully across the large stones in the stream which we crossed frequently, from one side to the other, along our trail. After a while we left the area where soft limestone predominated and found ourselves between basalt walls on each side. Basalt is a dark, heavy volcanic rock, formed when lava from eruptions eventually cools. We saw beautiful prism-like formations near the end of the canyon trail. It was there that the way became crowded with flower-gazers enjoying the views, not far from the arduous descent from the parking areas above the canyon.

After we huffed and puffed up the trail and out of the canyon, Gilad pointed out a "tell" below us. This mound, incongruously situated in the middle of the canyon below, was the site where a number of civilizations, dating back thousands of years, had existed. A tell is formed when the ruins of a settlement are used as a foundation for a subsequent settlement, and so on; layers of civilizations can be found at different strata. Tells in Israel are commonplace and many have been excavated, which is a very expensive practice. Consequently, only a fraction of tells will ever be fully explored and most of those chosen will relate to Jewish settlements rather than pagan or Christian ones.

We enjoyed the expansive view of the Jezreel Valley towards Mt. Tavor and the Mediterranean. Gilad explained the name of our location, Kochav (star) Heights. In ancient times a Jewish town named Kochav was sited nearby. The Crusaders built the Belvoir (beautiful view) fortress there. Later, Muslim forces headed by Saladin captured Belvoir, forcing the Crusaders to surrender in 1189. The Arab village Kawkab el-Hawa (star of the winds) was built over the ruins of the fortress in the 18th century. The Golani Brigade of the Israel Defense Forces conquered the village during the War of Independence, after defeating an Iraqi force on the slopes below. Many Jewish towns in Israel are named after Arab settlements, which were themselves named after older Jewish ones.

Completing our hike at Kibbutz Gazit, we walked through a magnificent orchard of blooming pink and white almond trees. The kibbutz was founded in 1947 by young immigrants from Turkey, Romania, and Poland. Not long after that, a large number of Zionist youths from Argentina arrived; sometimes Gazit is called the first Argentinian kibbutz. There are approximately 650 people living on the kibbutz, which makes its living from a wide variety of agricultural activities. There is also a large factory which produces various plastic products and employs kibbutz members and other workers from the surrounding area.

This hike in the Galilee, one of Israel's most beautiful regions, was very enjoyable. The memory of the gorgeous flower-laden fields will no doubt lure us back to Nahal Tavor in the future.

HIKING THE LOWER GALILEE

The locale of our recent ESRA hike was the Lower Galilee, near Mt. Atzmon. Unlike most of the Galilee, this area has a majority (60%) of Jews, with the rest of the population consisting of Arabs, Kurds, Circassians, and Beduin. It is a beautiful area with verdant views of the Jezreel and Kishon valleys and undulating hills.

Two thousand years ago, Israel was comprised of Judea, Samaria, and the Galilee - the most northern and largest region was the Galilee. From that time on, the local population was mixed between Jews, Christians (Jesus did some of his most significant wonders there), Arabs, Crusaders, more Jews (after the Inquisition), Ottoman Turks, the British, and yet more Jews and Muslims (since the late 19th century). Two of Galilee's large towns, Safed and Tiberias, became holy cities. In the early 20th century, the pioneering agricultural efforts which built up the country were made in the nearby Jezreel Valley, Israel's largest.

Our hike started from Kawkab el Hija, an Israeli Arab town that dates back to Crusader times. Kawkab (star in Arabic) el Hija is one of the "Al-Hija" villages named after the Kurdish warrior Hussam al-Din Abu al-Hija, who was commander of the Kurdish forces that took part in Saladin's conquest of the Crusader Kingdom from 1187 to 1193. It is said that Abu al-Hija, known as "the Daring" for his bravery, commanded the garrison of Akko at the time of Richard the Lionheart's siege of the city. Saladin rewarded Abu al-Hiza for his fortitude with the land on which Kawkab el Hija and other villages were founded.

In modern times, Kawkab el Hija had an enterprising mayor who provided excellent infrastructure for his town and had good relations with nearby Jewish communities, according to our knowledgeable guide Gidi. The main industry of the local Arabs is olive oil, for which the region has been famous for thousands of years. Gidi told us that Kawkab el Hija has a fierce rivalry with a nearby Israeli Arab town, Rumana, and that in 2006 the olive oil from both towns scored highly in international competition.

We hiked down the hill from Kawkab el Hija, first passing a sculpture garden with works by Jewish and Arab sculptors. We made our way through the Beit Netofa Valley towards Rumana and gradually began to climb Mt. Atzmon, which at 1,000 feet is the highest mountain in the Lower Galilee. After reaching the top of Mt. Atzmon and taking advantage of the fine view and the perfect weather to have a break, we descended into another valley before ascending once more towards the ancient city of Yodfat.

Yodfat was the birthplace of the mother of Amon, king of Judah (Kings 2, 21:21-22) "He [Amon] walked in all the ways of his father; he worshipped the idols his father had worshipped, and bowed down to them. He forsook the Lord, the God of his fathers, and did not walk in the way of the Lord." Not long after that, in 586 BCE, Judah fell to the Babylonians, who were said to be God's instrument to punish the idol-worshiping Jews. In the time of the Second Temple, the city was fortified by Joseph Ben Matityahu - the commander of the rebellion in Galilee, who held out heroically for 40 days. This was in the beginning of the Jewish Revolt against the Romans, 66-73 CE. The town's ruins reveal remains of buildings, caves, pools and pits from the Roman era.

The Roman siege of Yodfat was lengthy because of its double wall fortifications. Yodfat was the first of three fortified garrison towns to fall; the others were Gamla and Masada. As with Masada, the defenders had made a suicide pact in case of defeat. On the last day of the battle, Ben Matityahu and 40 of the surviving defenders fled to a cave, where they planned to commit suicide. But Ben Matityahu fixed the lots to be drawn so that his name would come out last. After the others killed themselves, he surrendered to the Romans. At the battle of Gamla, Ben Matityahu became a prisoner, but by the time of the epic battle at Masada, he had gone completely over to the Romans and had a new name, Flavius Josephus.

Josephus volunteered to write the history of the Great Revolt and General Vespasian, who later became emperor, agreed. So it was the turncoat Josephus who provided the Romans and posterity with a eyewitness account of the fall of Jerusalem in 70 CE. Of course, Josephus was writing for Vespasian, so in recent centuries his objectivity has been questioned.

Following the end of the war, Josephus was taken to Rome, where he wrote his history "The Jewish War". His second major work, "Jewish Antiquities", covered the time of Alexander the Great to the destruction of the Second Temple in 70 CE. Because of Josephus' reliance on hearsay and legend, historians had another reason to question the truthfulness of his writings.

Norma Franklin, one of the hikers who is an archeologist by training, updated the group on the validity of Josephus' works. Recent excavations have led to finds which are similar to what Josephus depicted. So, instead of his doubtful legitimacy as a historian, Josephus has gained a heightened stature in the eyes of contemporary scholars.

The most exciting and longest part of the hike ended after we climbed down from the remains of ancient Yodfat to the modern agricultural village below, with its beautiful fields and pastures. Gidi gave us the option of walking a few hours to meet the bus via a flat, rather unexciting route, or going directly to the bus. Honesty requires me to admit that Michal and I chose the latter option and spent a few hours finishing the weekend newspaper. Despite the anticlimactic ending, we found the hike to be very enjoyable and educational, as usual when hiking with ESRA.

See www.jewishvirtuallibrary.org for more information on Yodfat and Flavius Josephus.

GUIDED TOUR AT MEGIDDO

My wife Michal and I, part of a group of ten, recently had the pleasure of a personal tour of the Megiddo National Archeological Park, which overlooks the Jezreel Valley. Our guide to the UN-proclaimed site was our friend Dr. Norma Franklin, an archeologist who is the coordinator of the Megiddo Expedition of Tel Aviv University. (http://whc.unesco.org/en/list).

Mt. Megiddo was important in ancient times for its command of the Via Maris (Way of the Sea), one of the two principal routes connecting Egypt with the great empires of the Tigris-Euphrates Valley. (The other route is the King's Way through the mountains of Jordan.) Megiddo has three historical distinctions: first, it is the site of the world's first recorded battle; second, it is the site of the famous WWI victory of General Allenby against the Turkish Army; third, it is prophesied in the New Testament to be the site of the world's last battle - Armageddon.

Hieroglyphs depicting Pharaoh Thutmose III's victory over a combined force of Canaanite kings were inscribed on the walls of Egypt's Temple of Karnak after the first battle of Megiddo in 1457 BCE. The defeated armies from the powerful city-states were forced to flee to the stronghold of Mt. Megiddo, where they eventually succumbed to a lengthy siege. This was a momentous victory for Thutmose III. Egypt gained control of upper Canaan and recieved taxes and levies from the Assyrian, Babylonian, and Hittite kings to the north.

In the first half of 1918, German victories stymied the British forces in Palestine. But in mid-September, in the last of the great cavalry battles, General Edmund Allenby's forces broke the

Turkish line, opening a gap for Allenby's cavalry and ending any effective Turkish resistance as the Turks fled inland. Within five weeks, the Turks signed an armistice and Palestine was under British control. Allenby was later given the title of Lord Allenby of Megiddo.

The term Armageddon is a corruption of the Hebrew Har (mountain) and the Aramaic form of Megiddo - Megiddon. We know that the Book of Revelation (New Testament - Revelation 16:16) identifies Armageddon as the place where the armies of God and Satan will fight their ultimate battle. Because of all this history, the national park is a busy tourist destination for bus loads of Christian and Jewish tourists, in addition to Israelis out on weekend expeditions.

The UNESCO Advisory Body evaluation gives this explanation for Megiddo's choice as a World Heritage site: "Megiddo is one of the most impressive tells [earthen mound containing archeological remains] in the Levant [eastern Mediterranean coast]. It is strategically sited near the Aruna Pass [today also called Wadi Ara] and overlooks the fertile Jezreel Valley. Blessed with abundant water supplies, from the 7th millennium BCE through to the 4th century BCE Megiddo was one of the most powerful cities in Canaan and Israel. It controlled the Via Maris, the main international highway connecting Egypt to Syria, Anatolia and Mesopotamia. Epic battles that decided the fate of western Asia were fought nearby."

"Megiddo also has a central place in the biblical narrative, extending from the Conquest of the Land [by Joshua] through to the periods of the United and then Divided Monarchy and finally

Assyrian domination .... Megiddo is said to be the most excavated tell in the Levant. Its twenty major strata [levels] contain the remains of around 30 different cities ...."

"Megiddo represents a cornerstone in the evolvement of the Judeo-Christian civilization through its central place in the biblical narrative, its formative role in messianic beliefs, and for its impressive building works by King Solomon."

Our friend Norma had us jumping from century to century while exploring the more than twenty layers of the various time periods in the park. On one level we could have been standing next to a ruin from 3,500 BCE, while a few feet to the left and a few feet higher up, the period could have been a thousand years later. Norma explained how the shifting of the levels by natural phenomena, such as earthquakes, makes the identification of the ruins uncertain. The tell is complex and although it was continuously inhabited throughout the millennia, some areas were more densely occupied than others, which can easily confuse visitors.

Tel Megiddo has been undergoing excavations since 1903, prompting Norma to say she could have given us a three-day tour instead of one lasting only several hours. She gave us explanations of how earlier archeologists were at odds over some of the findings. Today, modern archeological methods rather than the biblical references are the main identifying criteria used.

Perhaps the best part, especially on a hot day like that of our visit, was exploring the enormous water system. We descended 30 meters down a steel stairway to a rocky platform. Then we walked through a tunnel large enough for several of us to traverse at a time. We marveled at the ancient technology that created this engineering feat with human-powered tools. While the Chicago archeological excavators who discovered the system in 1925 dated it to the Late Bronze period, around 1300 BCE, Yigal Yadin dated it five centuries later, during King Ahab's reign. Norma thinks it might date back to the Middle Bronze period, around 1600 BCE.

Many people regard Megiddo as the most important biblical period site in Israel. Its mighty fortifications, sophisticated water installations, impressive palaces and temples, and commanding height over the Via Maris highway assured its position as the "queen of cities" in Canaan and Israel. As we looked down from the heights of Tel Megiddo onto the modern highway which crossed the Jezreel Valley from Wadi Ara northwards - on the very route of the Via Maris - it wasn't hard to understand Megiddo's prominence in the ancient world. For more details about Megiddo, see the Tel Aviv University site. (http://megiddo.tau.ac.il/)

Afterwards, Norma took us to one of her favorite restaurants in the nearby Wadi Ara, where one of Israel's busiest roads - the same route used by Pharaoh Thutmose 3,500 years ago! - cuts through numerous Israeli-Arab towns. A very tasty finish to a wonderful tour.

THE FIRST DECADE – THE KIBBUTZ

Recently, we drove north with our usual traveling companions to see an art exhibition entitled "The First Decade: A Hegemony and a Plurality." Despite the pedantic title, we really enjoyed this overview of Israeli painting from 1948-1958. The Museum of Art at Kibbutz Ein Harod Meuchad was itself of great interest, as is the entire subject of kibbutz communities in Israel.

A form of communal living combining socialism and communism, the kibbutz has made an imprint on Israeli life far greater than its numbers would suggest. The first kibbutzim (pl.) were built by Jews who came to Israel during the Second Aliyah, a period of ten years which span from the outbreak of government-inspired pogroms in Russia - especially the Kishinev Pogrom - to the start of WWI. These new immigrants were inspired by a work ethic to build the Jewish state in Palestine with the labor of their own hands, a philosophy that was espoused by leaders such as A.D. Gordon (1856-1922).

Gordon came to Israel with his family when he was 48 and supported himself as a simple agricultural worker. In the evenings, after working in the fields, he toiled away on his philosophical texts, which became the inspiration for many newcomers to Palestine. Originally a member of the Love of Zion organization, Gordon eventually founded the Young Workers, a non-Marxist, Zionist movement which taught that physical labor on the land would redeem the Jews from having been "completely cut off from nature and imprisoned within city walls for two thousand years."

The early kibbutzim were built primarily on unused land in the Jezreel Valley, on the central coastal plain, or in the upper Jordan Valley. The kibbutzniks were extremely idealistic, expecting to live unexploited lives while not exploiting others. That is, they would work for themselves and employ no laborers. These early kibbutzniks were true communists, before the Communist Party even existed in Russia, and planned to work equally and share equally in the fruits of their labor. They were so idealistic that they even expected that the local Arab laborers who worked for the wealthy Arab landowners in Beirut and Cairo would welcome them.

The history of the kibbutzim is a woeful tale of farming swampy land, malaria and other sicknesses, fighting the Arabs, and lack of money. Despite initial failures, by 1948 kibbutz members constituted about 7.5 per cent of Israel's population. Prime Minister David Ben-Gurion's government supported the kibbutzim and they supplied many of the military and political leaders of the growing nation.

While branching out from agriculture to manufacturing (and later tourism), the kibbutzim remained true to their ideals, discouraging individual families from raising children on their own or even eating separately. Children's Houses and communal dining halls were symbols of this severe ideology. Eventually the economics of the modern age caught up with the kibbutzim, resulting in a dramatic decline in kibbutz membership by nearly two-thirds, following the failure of the Israeli economy in the 1980s. While kibbutzim are slowing rebuilding their status based on modern methods of management, a handful still cling to the original ideology on which the movement was built. Even so, many

Israelis who now live on kibbutz land are strictly householders, with no ownership of communal kibbutz property and enterprises.

We were on our way to Ein Harod Meuchad, established in 1921 in the expansive Jezreel Valley. It is one of Israel's first "green" kibbutzim, located near Mt. Gilboa and the Harod Spring. In 1953, Ein Harod split into Ein Harod Meuchad and Ein Harod Ihud, based on fierce ideological differences. Ironically, today the two Ein Harods are both members of the United Kibbutz Movement, one of several groupings in the kibbutz movement, and the ideology which caused the split is hardly remembered. The Art Museum on the kibbutz is the first dedicated art museum to be built in the Yishuv. It was built by the kibbutzniks in the 1930s, even before other essential needs were satisfied, because of their belief that culture and art are among the most basic formative constituents of a society.

The current art museum was gradually built over Israel's first decade. Its designer was Samuel Bickels, who trained as an architect in Europe before immigrating to Israel in the 1930s to escape burgeoning anti-Semitism, along with many other architects. The building's natural light results from sophisticated double roofs with clerestory windows, which allow for excellent illumination without the need for artificial lighting. (www.museumeinharod.org.il/english/about/)

To celebrate Israel's 60th anniversary, all six decades of Israeli art are being shown in six different venues around Israel. We were particularly happy to see this show because all of us prefer the earlier artists to the modern ones, who seem to us to be blatantly political. (Perhaps this concept is just a sign of our aging.) Most of the paintings and sculpture exhibited was by artists who had been active before Israel's Declaration of Independence in 1948. We saw a concise survey of early Israeli art, historically interesting, educational, and esthetically enjoyable. Some of the themes touched upon in the art works are socio-cultural issues of the founders of the state, Holocaust issues, Jewish and Arab immigration, the War of Independence, women artists, and among the most interesting, posters promoting the emergence of a collective national identity.

After having our fill of art, we toured Beit Sturman, a regional science museum located just one hundred yards down the road. During the informative introductory film we learned that the museum was named after a kibbutz notable, Haim Sturman, who was killed in 1938. Sturman was a friend and adviser to Orde Wingate, the famous British officer and Christian Zionist who organized and trained "Special Night Squads" which used guerilla tactics to stymie Arab attacks. Sturman's son, and later two grandsons, also fell in subsequent Arab-Israeli wars.

The museum's aim is to educate the region's children in local archeology, botany, and history. We particularly enjoyed seeing the extensive collection of Roman milestones and specimens of taxidermy in the botany exhibit. Afterwards, we repaired to a nearby fish restaurant, where we enjoyed an endless number of small salads, whole grilled fish, chips (the Israeli name for french fries) and dessert. An excellent day trip which couldn't have ended better.

HIKING THE SEAM IN GALILEE

We recently joined ESRA for an autumn hike along the Amud stream (middle and lower parts) in the Upper Eastern Galilee. The hike started from Ein Koves near the ancient city of Safed and traversed the middle and lower parts of Nahal Amud to Kibbutz Hukuk. As we traveled north on our bus from the coastal plain, we turned inland towards Lake Kinneret. We were passing through an area known for its olives when our excellent guide, Avishai, pointed out an interesting fact: olive trees rarely have two big harvests in a row. In alternate years, the trees consolidate their growth or put out fruit. Avishai explained that the rhythm of the olive trees allows them to exist for hundreds, if not thousands of years.

We passed a large reservoir belonging to Israel's water utility, Mekorot. One of the most advanced companies of its kind, Mekorot has enabled Israel to support a population of more than seven million in an arid country of which two-thirds is desert. Avishai educated us about the three major sources of natural water in Israel. The Kinneret is one of Mekorot's largest sources and is certainly Israel's most talked-about one. It receives the majority of its water from the Jordan River, the diversion of which has greatly reduced the river's flow southward from the Kinneret, to the detriment of the Dead Sea. Israelis hold their breath when the elevation of the Kinneret declines below its "red line", which has happened after years of less than average rainfall. There is even concern that the "black line" may be exceeded as well. If that happens, the giant pumps that transport the water from the lake, which is more than 600 ft. below sea level, to the National Water Carrier system of water channel pipes, won't function.

On a more positive note, we discussed the great progress in desalination Israel has made, with the world's largest reverse-osmosis desalination plant in Ashkelon among a total of 31 plants around the country, and more in the works. For example, in 2011 a huge seawater desalination plant, now under construction in Ashdod, will be operational. Of equal importance is the fact that Israel recycles a much higher proportion of its water than any other nation.

Israel also has the large Coastal and Mountain Aquifers, plus smaller underground lakes. Many of Israel's waters sources are in dispute with the Palestinian Authority. Consequently, besides the arid climate, pollution from increasing development, and burgeoning population pressure, there's a large political component to Israel's water problems. As some experts say, water may be the cause of future regional wars.

A steep descent led us to our trail, approximately midway along the long Nahal Amud (Amud stream). As Israel has had several relatively dry winters in a row, the bed of the stream (once, in centuries past, a river) was completely dry along our route. In any event, at this point we were about 500 ft. above the stream bed, on a lovely wooded trail (plane and jujube trees) with many man-made terraces, mostly eroded, overlooking the deep gorge with its limestone cliffs. At our first rest stop on one of the larger terraces, we talked about the civilization that had built the terraces here, after having advanced from hunter-gatherers to cultivators. Avishai described the ongoing conflict between cultivators (settled groups) and hunter-gatherers (nomads), exemplified by Arab and Jewish city-dwellers and villagers pitted against the Beduin nomads. Israel's southern and eastern neighbors, which also have large Beduin populations, have similar conflicts.

Along the stream bed, the remains of 18 disused mills, numerous bridges, and dams can still be found. During our lunch break, Avishai read to us from the historic document announcing the imminent expulsion of the Jews from Spain in 1492. He told us how this forced migration led to the flowering of the city of Safed as a center of Jewish learning and mysticism during the 16th century, Safed's golden age.

When the Jews were forced either to convert or leave Spain, nearly penniless, within three months after the decree, only one place welcomed them: the Ottoman Empire. Sultan Bayazid II understood the value of cultivating a middle class which would promote commerce through trade, banking, and diplomacy. The Jews were the obvious ones to fit this description, since they constituted the bulk of the middle class in Spain, had a wide network of coreligionists throughout the known world to trade with, were conversant in many languages, and had a rudimentary banking system. Some Jews settled in Adrianople, where they learned a more advanced way to fabricate fine woolens using the process of "fulling", a process which repeatedly beats the wool until the threads are very tight and the fabric shrinks to half its original size, turning it into felt.

Just 25 years after the expulsion from Spain (followed by a similar one from Portugal), the Ottomans conquered Palestine and the Sultan invited the Jews to move there to enrich the empire. Some came to Safed, to capitalize on the already existing terraces, flour mills, water channels, and bridges next to the Nahal Amud. There the Jews created a center for the production of high-quality woolen fabrics by converting the flour mills into fulling mills. The woolens were then exported to customers all over Europe. Rabbi David de Rossi, who visited Safed in 1535, wrote: "Many Jews are arriving all the time and the clothing [textile] business is growing every day... and every man and woman who works in wool at any trade will earn a good living."

But in 1576-77, Sultan Murad III, the first anti-Jewish Ottoman ruler, ordered the deportation of many of the Jews of Safed to Cyprus, leading to the decline of the woolen industry in the area. Eventually, Arabs became the majority of the inhabitants of Safed and the city didn't regain its Jewish majority until Israel's War of Independence.

There was a slow descent to the lower part of Nahal Amud. At that point the trail literally spans the seam between the Upper and Lower Galilee regions. Here, the limestone cliffs took on a positively spooky look, with caves and other openings simulating skulls with hollow eye-sockets and other phantasmagorical shapes. We saw where the National Water Carrier crossed the deep gorge towards the center of Israel. The water pipe, nearly 10 ft. in diameter, is encased in concrete and looks like the stairway of a giant Aztec pyramid. Just ahead of us, near the exit from the gorge, was the natural limestone column ("amud" in Hebrew) which gives the stream its name. Nearly 100 feet high, its top is shaped like a monolith from Easter Island. This was a fitting sight to climax our eight-mile hike, which is among the most beautiful we've done anywhere.

International style (Bauhaus) building, Tel Aviv

Western Wall, Old City, Jerusalem

Rockefeller Museum courtyard, Jerusalem

Carmel National Park

Tower and Stockade construction, Tel Amal (1936)

Bell Park - Tel Amal

Roman ruins, Bet She'an

Lower Galilee vista

Dead Sea vista - Ein Bokek

Steve and Michal at Nahal Oz

View of Masada from Mt. Elazar

Nabatean ruins at Shivta

Encountering Israel – the South

GETTING AWAY FROM IT ALL – THE DEAD SEA AND THE OLD CITY

There's always a lot to get away from: the economy, the latest pandemic, the impending end of the universe, etc. While many Israelis are content to spend nearly every weekend at home, we like to get away and explore the country, visit museums, relax by the sea, or just take a hike on a new or favorite trail. So, this past weekend we decided to enjoy ourselves in the Jerusalem area with friends.

We began by driving to one of the natural wonders of the world, the Dead Sea. The fact that the lowest place on earth is only an hour and a half from our home is a big plus. We drove by Jerusalem, past the large suburb of Ma'aleh Adumim, turned right when we were in sight of Jericho (the world's oldest city), and soon arrived at Mineral Beach.

Mineral Beach is a popular destination for day-trippers and tourists, including Christian groups, which constitute the majority of Israel's visitors. We saw many people covered in the special mud for which Mineral Beach is renowned. The black mineral-rich mud attracts crowds to bathe here, especially those from the former Soviet Union who are almost addicted to spas. In addition to floating in the sea, one can enjoy the covered sulfur pool, a freshwater pool, snack bar, showers and dressing rooms. We enjoyed the changing colors of the mountains on both sides of the Dead Sea as the day wore on and we finally prepared to return to Jerusalem, Israel's capital.

Jerusalem's Regency Hotel is on Mt. Scopus next to the Hebrew University. Perched above the Old City, it has an unparalleled view of both the ancient and the new parts of Jerusalem. Its architecture is unique, modeled on an ancient terraced palace and it contains probably the best hotel health club in Israel. We enjoyed an excellent Shabbat dinner and got ready for our hike on Saturday morning.

We have circumnavigated the walls of the Old City on several Tisha B'av evenings (a day of mourning, known as the worst day in Jewish history), a new tradition which attracts many people each year. On those walks we have always been intrigued by the illuminated tombs and churches of the Kidron Valley, which runs alongside the southern wall of the Old City. We decided to explore this area by day.

We made our way down to the valley through David's City, which the Arabs call Silwan. David's City has become a hub for Jewish and Christian tourists interested in exploring Jerusalem's most ancient archeological attractions. Though mostly populated by Arabs, there are scores of Jewish families who live in Jewish-owned properties in David's City. These families have bought land and reclaimed it for its ancestral owners, the Jews.

Having looked at the water sources in David's City, which were once crucial for Jerusalem's survival, we entered the Kidron Valley, part of the burial belt for Jerusalem of the Second Temple period. There are many unmarked ancient graves, as well as thousands of modern burial sites. We saw Absalom's Monument, the Tomb of the Sons of Hezir, and Zechariah's Tomb, each of which dates back thousands of years. Further along, we saw the tear-shaped Diminus Flevit Church, the Mary Magdalene Church, with its gorgeous, gold cupolas, and the Church of All Nations. We entered the Tomb of Mary Church, which is buried below ground, a cool rest stop after our trek. We then concluded our hike by walking on the path adjacent to the walls of the Old City.

Following a sumptuous lunch at the hotel, the afternoon was spent by the pool and at the health club, then cocktails on the balcony at sunset. While we only booked the hotel for Friday night, the custom in Israel is to remain at the hotel until Shabbat ends in the evening. We stayed until sunset, then hurried out for a quick supper near Zion Square before attending a concert at the Israel Museum. Larry Willis, a great American jazz pianist, was accompanied by two excellent Israeli sidemen, a drummer and a bass player. A most enjoyable conclusion to a great weekend!

There is something about Jerusalem: if you don't feel it in your heart, if you don't resonate to its history, if you don't thrill to walk on the cobble stones of our heritage, you are missing out on perhaps Israel's greatest attraction. We felt it, we resonated with it, and we certainly walked it. Having gotten away from it all, we were ready to begin a new week.

VACATIONING IN MITZPE RAMON AND TIBERIAS

Mitzpe Ramon is situated at the edge of Machtesh Ramon, the largest machtesh in the world: 25 miles long by 5 miles wide, with a depth of 1,250 feet. Located in the Negev Desert, which comprises most of the lower portion of Israel, the huge crevasse reminds one of a much smaller version of the Grand Canyon. On a recent trip to Mitzpe Ramon we stopped beforehand at "Neve Midbar" Hot Springs Desert Spa, whose facilities include numerous indoor and outdoor pools, a restaurant and ample changing and shower facilities.

In Mitzpe Ramon, we stayed at an outstanding hotel, the Ramon Inn. From its looks and especially its ambiance, it would be hard to guess that this hotel had been converted from two adjoining apartment blocks. (A new facility is currently being built.) Its outstanding cuisine included unusual spices and combinations, exquisitely prepared, which really made the meals delightful. Adding to our enjoyment of the area was a sunset walk along the sculpture garden / promenade adjacent to the crater's edge, where we enjoyed wine and cheese. The town has a futuristic tourist center overlooking the crater that many people visit, even if they are just stopping off on the way to Eilat.

Spread before us was the Machtesh Ramon, the largest of three examples in Israel. The Hebrew term "machtesh" is a geological one which means "mortar", as in mortar and pestle. While there are a few small, un-named machteshim (pl) elsewhere, the machtesh is generally known as a unique feature of Israel. The word is sometimes mistranslated as "crater", but there is an important difference. A machtesh is caused by erosion only, has one or two "wadis" (dry river beds) leading to the entrance/exit, and takes a hundred million years or more to form. By comparison, there is no crucial time factor in the creation of a crater, which can be caused by a meteor or may be just a hole in the ground. The Small and Large Machteshim were rediscovered in modern times (1942) by Jewish explorers. Ironically, they were unaware of the largest machtesh further south, which was subsequently named "Machtesh Ramon", from the Arabic word for Roman.

We took a four-hour jeep tour of the machtesh on our first morning and then returned there the next day for a three-hour hike, finishing up with tea, pita and salads at a Beduin tent. Also in the same area is Sde Boker, the kibbutz where David Ben-Gurion spent the last years of his life. The cottage where he and his wife Paula lived is fascinating, while the graves of the "first family" of modern Israel overlook the Wilderness of Zin, another incredible tourist site. Not far away are the ruins of the Nabatean city of Avdat, a powerful city state which flourished along the spice route in the last centuries before the Common Era.

More recently, we traveled up north to the Galilee region. We stayed in Tiberias, on Lake Kinneret, and were happy to see the resurgence of the large lake to its former proportions. Due to the drought conditions of the last several years, the beach surrounding the lake had increased in size to the point that hundreds of yards of sand and vegetation were exposed as the water dwindled. At that time the lake was again full, after an especially rainy winter. This event was so unexpected that a brand new beach, built especially for the ultra-Orthodox desirous of separate bathing facilities, was submerged by the resurgent waters. Since then, further drought conditions have once again lowered the water to a dangerous level, endangering a major part of Israel's water supply.

We stayed at the Carmel Jordan River Hotel, which was once the premier resort hotel in town, frequented by Israel's elite. During our stay it was somewhat neglected (it has since been restored to its former glory). Unlike most of the other tourist destinations in Israel, Tiberias, one of Judaism's four holy cities, had no hotel building boom in the run-up to the second millennium. Walking around the town, it's almost like returning to the Israel of 40-50 years ago, with falafel and shwarma stands, sandal shops, and small stores and cafés everywhere, all of which add to Tiberias' faded charm.

On the first day of the weekend we left early for the nearby Golan Heights, where we had a delightful time picking all the cherries and assorted berries that we could eat in the Bustan (orchard) of the Golan. We wandered through the orchards for a few hours, took a tractor ride to the border opposite Syria, and enjoyed coffee and Druze pita with labaneh, a yogurt spread. Then we left the Golan and went to Kibbutz Kfar Blum, where we kayaked down the Hatzbani and Jordan Rivers. We had a leisurely afternoon lunch at an inn along the road on our way back to Tiberias. That evening we walked along the lakeside promenade and had a reasonably priced fish dinner at one of the restaurants.

The next day, after touring some of the old city, we drove to a lakeside beach associated with the hotel. We swam and relaxed in the shade for several hours, enjoying the cool water and breezes. The Kinneret is far below sea level, the lowest lake of its size in the world except for the Dead Sea. It's a great favorite of vacationing Israelis, perfect for swimming, boating, and camping.

Before leaving the area we stopped at sensational Bet Gavriel, a cultural center built on the lake shore, which is devoted to the humanities: music, drama, dance, cinema, etc. It is also the location of international and regional conventions, including the peace conference where the treaty between Israel and Jordan was signed. Apart from all this, the buildings and grounds are exquisite. The café located on the site lived up to its location, so we enjoyed another excellent and inexpensive meal before returning home.

HEADING SOUTH TO EILAT

Early one morning, we headed south with friends for Israel's southernmost city, Eilat. After an hour and a half we were on the outskirts of Beersheba, a large city of a few hundred thousand. Perched at the edge of the desert, Beersheba has grown rapidly in the last few decades. With frequent, speedy train service to Tel Aviv, a first class university, much high-tech industry, and a vibrant population with many new immigrants from many lands, Beersheba's future seems bright.

We were surprised to see the lovely neighborhoods adjacent to the Israeli Air Force Museum, which was our first destination. The museum covers much ground, with more than 150 planes on display from all periods of Israel's modern history. There is a small museum with very interesting displays and photographs, but we had the most fun just strolling through the huge array of planes. Among the most interesting were tiny planes used by the fledgling air corps during the War of Independence, the jets (mostly bought from France) with which Israel vanquished Russia's MiG fighter jets, and some of the MiGs which Arab defectors flew to Israel.

We continued south past the Dead Sea and through the Arava Desert. It was here that the magnificent red-tinged mountains of Jordan became our constant companion to the east, just across the desert plain. One can compare this route to a condensed version of a drive through the Western deserts of North America — in only three hours! With the Moabite and Edomite Mountains on the left and a similar range on our right in Israel itself, we swiftly covered the distance to the northern shore of the Red Sea, passing a few kibbutzim on the way, but not much else.

Before we moved to Israel, I had thought that Eilat was something like Miami Beach, but much closer to central Israel than Florida is to the Mid-Atlantic States. I got the last part correct, but the climate of Eilat is not at all similar to the southern coast of Florida. Though it is located at the northern tip of the Red Sea, Eilat is surrounded on all other sides by desert or mountains. Foremost is the Israel's Negev Desert, but Eilat is also adjacent to Jordanian and Egyptian deserts and the Saudi Arabian peninsula is easily visible to the southeast. There's almost no rainfall there and no humidity. The summer temperatures are similar to Arizona, with 100-degree days common.

Pulling into Eilat is always a treat, with new hotels and lagoons to explore on every visit. Eilat is a resort city, with some features similar to Las Vegas or Atlantic City, our hometown, but it's much smaller and there's no gambling. We went directly to the Sport Hotel, part of the Isrotel chain, which has seven or eight hotels in Eilat alone.

While the weather in Eilat is usually dry and pleasant, the rain which was falling up north accompanied us most of the way and even fell intermittently in Eilat for a day and a half. As a consequence, we went to the mall on Friday for something to do. It was like Black Friday (the Friday after Thanksgiving) in America! The shopping center was jammed, with standing-room-only in some stores. Because Eilat is the sole city in Israel exempted from the national VAT (value added tax), many visitors shop for expensive items while there, making the centrally located mall Israel's busiest per square foot. That night we attended a very entertaining casino-type show at another Isrotel hotel, at a reduced price. It was almost like being in Atlantic City.

By Saturday the weather had cleared. We took a long walk around the hotel district, skipping the very muddy hiking trails. We walked past the grand hotels and ended up along the Red Sea shore at a much more humble location: the original British police station which Israeli troops captured during the War of Independence. There we found a statue similar to the American statue commemorating Iwo Jima, but here the flag being raised was hand-colored with ink. By capturing the police station, Israel gained a Red Sea port which has proven to be invaluable for trade with Asia, eliminating the need for ships to pass through the Suez Canal to get here. In 1949, when the "ink flag" was raised, there was practically no other construction along the seashore. What a difference today!

We enjoyed some boat rides in the afternoon: a "speed boat" and a paddleboat, both of which traveled at about the same speed — slow. It was enjoyable nonetheless. We returned to the hotel for yet another trip to the jacuzzi, while I took advantage of the excellent fitness room. There was still time for a drink by the pool and a light supper before we left our friends and headed to the airport, just a five-minute taxi ride away. One of the best things about Eilat is how close it is to the rest of the country. After the short, 35-minute flight, we quickly arrived back home in Alfe Menashe, which seemed a world away from the desert and sea of Israel's Red Sea resort.

BITTERSWEET DAYS, THE DEAD SEA AND EN GEDI

It was a great week in Israel, punctuated by my birthday coinciding with Independence Day. Of course, the run-up to Independence Day is solemn, because our Memorial Day to our fallen soldiers and victims of terror precedes it. In America, Memorial Day has become commercialized, devoted as much to big sales in the shopping centers as it is to commemorating the dead. The American Jewish community celebrates Yom Hazikron (Day of Remembrance) based on convenience, rather than coupling it with Independence Day. How different from the Israeli custom, which binds the two ceremonies together inseparably.

It was a stroke of Israeli genius that linked the bitter and the sweet to ensure that we don't take our freedom in this land for granted. The major ceremony at the national cemetery on Mt. Herzl and the hundreds of smaller ones in every community on the eve of our Memorial Day are crowded. Nearly everyone takes the time to remember the sacrifices that have been made, and continue to be made, to ensure our independence. The eerie siren at 8:00 in the evening brings (almost) everyone to attention, with heads bowed. The next day, the same siren at 10:00 in the morning halts all traffic, vehicular and pedestrian, and all work, as we again stand to sear into our memories the fate of the fallen, victims of both "organized" war and terrorism.

No one is given the day off for the Israeli Memorial Day. It is not intended to be a day to shop or go to the beach. But by the late afternoon the mood begins to swing towards exhilaration, as people get off work early to head home. At 8:00 in the evening, Independence Day is ushered in. Some say that the abrupt transition from a somber mood to a joyous one is difficult for those who are bereaved. No doubt that is true, but at the same time nearly everyone in Israel has a family member or a close friend to mourn.

So, the celebratory mood of the eve of Independence Day is a must for us. The dead are not forgotten, but the emphasis switches to joyous festivity. As usual, our town put on a terrific show, using only local talent, unlike many other communities who hire celebrities. This year the entertainment was a tribute to all the different branches of the Israel Defense Forces. Besides the great fireworks, the highlight for me is the incredible dancing, which involves many corps of young girls (and a few boys) from primary school through high school age. At the end of the evening, as the fireworks display climaxes and all the performers are on the stage singing the Alfe Menashe anthem, it's impossible not to feel a tremendous surge of pride in everything that our small country has accomplished in just six-plus decades.

This year, for the holiday, instead of going to a museum or to an army base, we headed to the Dead Sea for a long weekend. We arrived at the Hod Hotel at En Bokek in time for dinner with our friends. A 4-star hotel, the Hod is built right on the beach by the Dead Sea. It's one of the original tourist hotels built in En Bokek, which now has dozens.

The next morning, following the sumptuous Israeli breakfast (salads, breads, quiches, eggs, smoked fish, cakes, fruit, yogurts, etc.) we headed to nearby En Gedi National Park, a beautiful nature reserve which is an oasis in the Judean Desert. Although leopards (almost extinct), wolves, foxes, and hyenas are found in the reserve, what hikers see most are small herds of horned ibex and the Rock hyrax, a small mammal. Both species are excellent climbers, a necessity in this mountainous terrain.

We started our hike at 1,300 feet below sea level, taking the relatively easy path to the En Gedi Spring. We cooled our feet in the natural pool at the foot of the waterfall, then continued upward to Shulamit's Spring. This is where David is said to have hidden out more than 3,000 years ago, after King Saul sent his men to slay him. We all recall the story of the shepherd boy David who slew the Philistine giant Goliath. It is said that after the victory hundreds of Saul's soldiers paid tribute to the king, but thousands paid tribute to David. This incensed the king and David fled. "And David went up from thence, and dwelt in the strongholds of En Gedi." (Samuel I 23:29)

We then skirted around the edges of the cliffs on a narrower trail, reaching Dodim's Cave, another spot where David is said to have found shelter. We ate our sandwiches (made by us at breakfast) at David's Falls, a beautiful, scenic spot. Eventually we returned to the hotel, where we enjoyed the pool and bathing in the Dead Sea. We also enjoyed shopping for some of the diverse cosmetic products made from the local Dead Sea minerals, featured in many stores in the town.

In the evening, the lobby entertainment area was packed to hear a singer from Dimona's Black Hebrew community. This group, who believe themselves to be descended from Judeans exiled in 70 CE, is a sect which was established in Israel decades ago by a charismatic leader from Chicago. (Black Hebrews are classified as permanent residents, though some have received Israeli citizenship.)

On Shabbat (Saturday), there was more lounging on the beach and floating in the Dead Sea, an effortless feat for anyone. We also took advantage of the excellent spa at the hotel, with its fitness room and many varieties of massages.

The next day, for my birthday, we arranged in advance for five donkey carts to meet us in the desert. Our group was very surprised when we came upon the donkeys in the desert. We got on board and drove the carts to the middle of nowhere. There our guide and her Beduin helper set up a shade tent and served tea and pita bread, which had been prepared on the fire alongside of the tent. With the pita came lebaneh, a sour milk spread common in the Middle East - delicious! We enjoyed the cart rides much more than our previous experiences with donkeys, which had consisted of riding on the donkey's back.

While our friends headed back to the hotel for some more swimming, Michal, her sister, Linda, and I drove about 2.5 hours home to celebrate my birthday with our son Shaul, who had been given special leave from army duty in Hebron. We went to a popular grill restaurant for dinner, a type of Middle Eastern restaurant which Israelis love. In fact, there were four other families celebrating birthdays there!

There's a lot that's great about life in this small country, despite the bittersweet existence that we experience. For me, having a big birthday coincide with Independence Day made it even more significant. As they say in Israel on one's birthday: Live until 120!

BEN-GURION'S DREAM – THE NEGEV

"The Negev is one of the Jewish nation's safe havens," is a famous quote of Israel's legendary first prime minister, David Ben-Gurion. The Negev Desert was the love of Ben-Gurion's life, second only to the State of Israel. Ben-Gurion and his wife Paula joined the Sde Boker kibbutz in the Negev in 1953 and moved there after his retirement from politics. Ben-Gurion chose to spend the remaining years of his life as an "ordinary" kibbutz member living in a modest cottage. His monument and his and his wife's graves are grandly situated on a bluff overlooking the Wilderness of Zin, a fantastic site alongside of the road to Israel's southernmost city, Eilat.

The Negev Desert comprises about 60% of the land of the small country of Israel, with only about 8% of Israel's 7-plus million people. The result is that the northern sector of Israel is about equal in density to the Netherlands, the West's most densely populated country. Ben-Gurion correctly foresaw that Israel must take advantage of the Negev's wide open spaces to accommodate the millions of Jews that he hoped would eventually reside here.

Beersheba is the largest city in the Negev region and in fact, one of Israel's biggest with its population of 200,000. Although most of the Negev was included in the 1947 UN Partition Plan for Palestine, Beersheba – where the patriarch Abraham watered his flocks of sheep – was not. It became part of the modern State of Israel during the War of Independence. Beersheba is home to Ben-Gurion University of the Negev and Soroka Hospital, one of Israel's leading research and teaching hospitals. The city is connected to the Tel Aviv metropolitan area by a popular train line, which has reduced travel time enough to allow commuting between the two areas. Currently the traffic is mostly from Beersheba to Tel Aviv, but the aim of the Negev 2015 plan is to make the daily exchange of workers less one-sided.

The government has partnered with the Jewish Agency and the Jewish National Fund to implement "Negev 2015". With a budget of $4 billion, the plan envisions the doubling of Beersheba's population with about 25 satellite towns surrounding it. A similar explosion of town building is planned for Eilat, which is now primarily a resort destination. The smaller town of Mitzpe Ramon, next to the unique Ramon Crater, is destined to have about 17 satellite towns. As these developments are built, the Negev will become a magnet for businesses and families looking for more space and reduced expenses, both of which will be available according to "Negev 2015".

A major input to the importance of the Negev is the expected movement to that area of most of Israel's large military establishment. The nascent Training Base City will cover a huge area of undeveloped land, freeing up valuable real estate in the north. The families of military personnel and the businesses needed to service them will necessarily move to the south, adding to the population. As property costs continue to rise up north, the Negev's open spaces will beckon medium and large businesses to relocate.

The Negev's development will, of course, impact heavily on Israel's Jewish population, who will spread out from the Tel Aviv-Jerusalem-Haifa metropolitan areas where most Israelis live today. Perhaps even more affected will be the Beduin citizens of Israel, who are about 25-30% of the Negev's 500,000+ population. (At the time of the War of Independence in 1948 there were about 10,000 Beduin in the Negev.) Israel has a very high population growth for a Western country. But Negev Beduin are among the most fertile peoples on Earth, with families of ten children or more; many Beduin men have more than one wife.

Like other nomad civilizations, the Beduin abhor borders which inhibit their age-old grazing patterns. The Israeli Beduin once wandered all over the territories of Jordan, Israel, and the Sinai Peninsula, but they have been increasingly constrained by all the neighboring governments in recent decades. In Israel, there are seven recognized towns set up by the government for the Beduin. But there are another 45 unrecognized towns, which usually have no electricity or other modern conveniences, though they may have piped in water. Ten of these towns recently were officially recognized and can expect some improvements in infrastructure from the government.

There is a large percentage of unemployment among the Beduin, despite the facts that many Beduin students attend Ben-Gurion University and that Beduin men are able to join the Israeli army. Unfortunately the Beduin have not been served well by the government, but one hopes that they will be able to cope with the developing Negev and accommodate themselves to the changes.

Of course, there are others who are unhappy about the prospects of a vastly developed Negev region. Environmentalists prefer that things stay the same, but Israel's population is growing rapidly. And if Jews do not increasingly populate the Negev, it will eventually be taken over by the Beduin, with their extreme growth rate of approximately 5%. So, not only must Israel increase the number of Jews in the Negev for economic and geographic reasons, it has to encourage Jewish development for nationalistic and demographic ones. There are practical ways to do this, to benefit both Jews and Beduin. For example, increased educational and employment opportunities for the Beduin will increase their wellbeing and will inevitably result in a lower birthrate - which has proven to be a big factor in upgrading women's' rights around the world.

The Negev is home to some of the worlds' most advanced research in agriculture, water conservation, and solar energy. The hope for the Negev is that intelligent planning and attention paid to long-term environmental needs will result in a blooming desert, just as David Ben-Gurion dreamed. One hundred years after he made aliyah to Israel, Ben-Gurion's plans may be coming to fruition.

A DEAD SEA HIKE AND GUSH ETZION

Recently we traveled to the Dead Sea area, a great place to go in winter for pleasant hiking and touring. (Once June arrives, it's way too hot!) We joined the ESRA hiking group and rode in a comfortable bus past Beersheba, through the Negev Desert to the Judean Desert, and then descended to the Zohar ravine, our hike's starting point. From there we had a fantastic view of the Dead Sea's southern sector as well as the Masada plateau, where Jewish zealots killed themselves rather than surrender to Roman soldiers after the sacking of Jerusalem.

Technically, the southern sector of the Dead Sea is devoid of water. The sea, which loses 1.5 to 3 feet of water each year, has been devastated by both natural and industrial forces. The Jordan River, which feeds into the sea, has been diverted in places by both Israel and Jordan, leaving it barely more than a stream. This prevents the lake from replenishing itself after naturally-occurring evaporation. In addition, the Israeli and Jordanian Dead Sea industrial works exploit the Dead Sea without sufficient regard for its survival. The southern sector has been turned into an industrial site: many artificial pools with crisscrossing access roads. Burgeoning tourist facilities at En Bokek add to the environmental problems.

The northern sector of the sea, where there are no hotels and less industrial devastation, also attracts tourists, though there are problems of erosion and sinkholes. While various schemes have been proposed to shunt water into the Dead Sea, from either the Red Sea or the Mediterranean, political roadblocks have prevented their implementation. This is a shame, since international funds are available for a joint Israeli-Jordanian effort, which would provide many jobs and ensure the Dead Sea's "vitality". Currently, the World Bank and other organizations are investigating the consequences of a Red Sea - Dead Sea canal.

We entered the Zohar ravine from the overlook and quickly came upon a small fortress which was built and later abandoned by the Nabatean civilization. The Nabateans were Arabs who spoke Aramean and were devoted to trading, not agriculture or war. With no securely defined boundaries, their trading network was connected by strings of oases in which they built settlements, the largest of which was Petra. They traded mostly in perfume (frankincense and myrrh) used extensively at that time in the religious temples to counteract the odors from the daily animal sacrifices, as well as bitumen (pitch) from the Dead Sea. Eventually, the Nabateans were overrun by the Roman civilization and converted to Christianity, leaving very little cultural history to record their passing.

We continued our hike through Nahal Yizrach and Nahal Rom, two dry river beds which are typical of the crevasses common in this area of the Syria-Africa Rift. This narrow part of the Rift, which goes from Asia down to Africa, is only about 35 miles wide. The shifting of the tectonic plates caused by the frequent earthquakes here have created a variety of hiking trails, which can be a few hundred feet wide, with open vistas, or narrow and rocky. At lunch time we stopped at an incredible site, which looked far down onto a desolate, moon-like landscape, while at our back was a gorgeous view of the Dead Sea. Luckily our group was totally alone during the break, which added to this dramatic experience.

During the latter part of the walk the trail narrowed to a few yards, so that the rock walls towered over our heads as we scrambled carefully over the boulders and made our way down to the Dead Sea shore, about 1300 feet below "sea level". We met the bus and had time for either a quick float in the Dead Sea, or a cup of coffee on a sunny terrace, before heading back north to civilization.

Our appetites whetted by that great hike, we and our four friends headed south again the next weekend. This time we traveled through the Ayalon Valley, the location of many biblical and more contemporary battles, past hilly Beit Shemesh to the more mountainous Gush Etzion area. This bloc of communities is located in Judea (West Bank) between Jerusalem and Hebron, not far from Bethlehem. The almond trees were gloriously in bloom, as were the red anemones which carpeted the fields on either side of the road. We couldn't resist stopping the car and taking a romp through the flowers, which are even more dramatic when viewed on foot than from a passing vehicle.

In Gush Etzion, Jewish villages were built before the 1948 War of Independence to defend the southern approach to Jerusalem from invading armies. Historically, "it was here that Abraham and Isaac passed through on their sojourn from Hebron to Mount Moriah (Jerusalem), in its pastoral landscape Ruth gathered the sheaves from the fields of Bethlehem, upon its hilltops David shepherded his father's sheep and then went on to proclaim his kingdom, and in its deep caves the Maccabees and the Jewish fighters of Bar Kochba sought shelter." (www.judaica.org.il/history)

The modern Jewish settlement of Gush Etzion began in 1927 but harsh physical conditions forced the settlers to abandon their efforts. In 1935, the village of Kfar Etzion was established. This time repeated Arab attacks drove the pioneers away. Finally, in 1943 four communities were successfully built, only to be totally destroyed in 1948 by the Arabs, who killed 240 men and women and took 260 survivors as prisoners. Later that year, Prime Minister Ben-Gurion eulogized the defenders of Gush Etzion and their heroic stand against the Jordanian Legion: "I can think of no battle in the annals of the Israel Defense Forces which was more magnificent, more tragic or more heroic than the struggle for Gush Etzion .... If there exists a Jewish Jerusalem, our foremost thanks go to the defenders of Gush Etzion."

Israel retook the area in the 1967 Six Day War. This fact causes, some people to question whether Gush Etzion is legitimately part of Israel or whether it should be "given back" to the Palestinian Arabs. The Palestinian claim of sovereignty is based on the Jordanian conquest of 1948-1967. However, Israel is the last conqueror, which is the basis for national boundaries today throughout the world, such as between America and Mexico or France and Germany. Today, Gush Etzion is a crucial security buffer for Jerusalem and is only a ten-minute commute away. It includes more than a dozen dynamic and thriving communities and has a Jewish population of more than 20,000.

KING HEROD'S SUMMER PALACE AND MORE

We recently traveled south through the Gush Etzion area, just a short distance south of Jerusalem, to the Herodion (or Herodium) National Park. King Herod the Great, who reigned for the comparatively long period of 34 years, was the second son of Antipater the Idumaean, who founded the Herodian dynasty, and his wife Cypros, a Nabatean princess. While the Idumaeans had been converted to Judaism a short time before, Herod's claim to being a Jew was tenuous since his mother was a gentile. The family hobnobbed with the nobles in Rome, which resulted in Antipater being appointed Procurator over Judea. He then appointed Herod, only 25, to be the governor of Galilee.

At this time Rome ruled the known world and exacted taxes and obedience from its vassal states. Unlike all its other conquests, Judea was exempted from worshipping the Roman gods, but this privilege required the Jews to pay a special tax. The Romans accorded Judea a large measure of self-rule, of which Herod later took full advantage. Following his father's murder, Herod banished his first wife and married the teenage daughter (Mariamne) of the Hasmonean dynasty, the titular rulers of Judea.

In 40 BCE the Parthians invaded Judea and Herod fled to Rome. There he was made King of Judea by Mark Antony. Within three years Herod regained military control in Judea and began his remarkable reign, with backing from the Romans and by virtue of the Hasmonean (descendants of the Maccabees) bloodline flowing from his wife.

Herod used the great wealth generated by the trade routes which traversed Judea to build massive projects. In addition to the site we were exploring - the summer palace at Herodion - Herod built the port of Caesarea named after his patron in Rome, the fortress-palace at Masada opposite the Dead Sea, and his masterpiece, the magnificent enlargement of the Second Temple in Jerusalem. Unfortunately, Herod was something of a monster as well as a master builder. He had his wife and mother-in-law killed, as well as his brother-in-law and at least one of his sons. When he died in 4 BCE, his three remaining sons fought over their inheritance. Within two generations, Rome turned on Judea, burned the city of Jerusalem, and banished the Jews from their holiest city.

The palace at Herodion was constructed on top of a man-made mountain, to catch the winds off the desert as well as the magnificent views. It was divided into two sections: Upper Herodion, which contained the palace set within a circular fortress, and Lower Herodion, at the base of the mountain, which had numerous annexes for the use of the king's family and friends. The system of water storage was very sophisticated, with huge cisterns to supply the needs of the palace, including a large pool in Lower Herodion suitable for boating.

Not long after our visit, Professor Ehud Netzer of Hebrew University uncovered the grave of King Herod on the slope of the hill, not in the Tomb Estate which Herod had constructed for that purpose. "The approach to the burial site was via a monumental flight of stairs 6.5 meters wide, leading to the hillside; the stairs were especially constructed for the funeral procession. Herod died in Jericho, but left instructions to be buried in the area known as the Herodion. The mausoleum itself was almost totally dismantled in ancient times, but part of its well-built podium remains. Spread among the ruins are pieces of a large, unique coffin, nearly 2.5

meters (over 8 feet) made of a Jerusalemite reddish limestone, decorated with rosettes." (www.israelnationalnews.com)

Herodion was abandoned after being sacked by the Romans following the fall of Jerusalem, but in 132 CE it was occupied by Bar Kochba, the great Jewish general. Bar Kochba utilized the cisterns at Herodion for his guerilla attacks on the Roman army. Our group of six ascended the mountain through the cistern, in tunnels inside the mountain built to enable Bar Kochba's bands to make surprise attacks against the Romans. Tactics like this resulted in Bar Kochba's incredibly successful but short-lived victory over the Romans. Bar Kosiba (his original name) was given the nickname Bar Kochba (Son of a Star) and proclaimed *Messiah* by many Jews. "At the time, Bar Kochba - who was a man of tremendous leadership abilities – managed to unite the entire Jewish people around him. Jewish accounts describe him as a man of tremendous physical strength, who could uproot a tree while riding on a horse. This is probably an exaggeration, but he was a very special leader and undoubtedly had messianic potential, which is what Rabbi Akiva recognized in him." www.aish.com/literacy/jewishhistory)

But within three years, despite great victories against the Romans, the tide turned against the Jews. It is said that Bar Kochba became arrogant, listened too much to those who were proclaiming him Messiah, and relied too much on himself, forgetting the power of God. More cities were burned and left desolate, and the Jews, defeated and dispersed, never again threatened Rome's power.

On our way down from the mountain-top citadel, a plaque on the small office which once served as the park's toll booth reminded us of the battles modern Jews still fight in our ancient land. The plaque was inscribed in honor of the park ranger who had been murdered by Palestinians while on duty collecting admission charges. "I will restore My people Israel. They shall rebuild ruined cities and inhabit them; They shall plant vineyards and drink their wine; They shall till gardens and eat their fruits. And I will plant them upon their soil, nevermore to be uprooted from the soil I have given them." (Amos 9.14/15)

In the spirit of that blessing we left the park and visited the nearby Gush Etzion Winery, a recent business venture which uses grapes grown nearby. While in the shop we were joined by two other small groups of English-speakers. Many of the residents of Gush Etzion are Orthodox Jews from America, who are among the most Zionistic citizens in Israel.

We then traveled past Jerusalem and Ma'aleh Adumim to a Dead Sea beach and spent several hours soaking in the buoyant water, while enjoying the sight of the reddish Moabite Mountains shimmering in the distance. Joining us were busloads of Christian groups from America, Europe, and Japan. A short distance away was our lodging at Kibbutz Almog, where we had very nice, reasonably priced mini-suites. We enjoyed a typical Shabbat dinner in the dining hall, which is appropriately decorated to attract many religious families on weekends.

In the morning we hiked into the fantastic Nahal Og, a dry river bed which has trails similar to our previous weekend's location. The hike climaxed with narrow, steep crevices which had drops of thirty feet or more. No, we didn't jump down them, but used the "ladders" affixed to the rock walls to negotiate our way. While we enjoyed the steep descents - where one often couldn't see the next foothold - it definitely wasn't a hike for the unadventurous. Nevertheless, we encountered several large groups of hikers, including many families with small children, which entailed a bit of waiting at the steepest declines.

After returning to our rooms for much-needed hot showers, we made record time returning home via Jerusalem's new by-pass road. In less than an hour and a half we were at an Israeli-Arab restaurant close to home, enjoying the huge array of salads and grilled meats which were served at very reasonable prices. It'd been another great weekend to appreciate the many attractions which make Israel such a wonderful place to visit – or live in!

THE ZEALOTS TRAIL - MASADA

It was a fabulous day for a hike: early January, sun shining, cool temperature, and a perfectly clear sky. Our ESRA group made its first stop at a café/service station overlooking the Dead Sea, the lowest place on Earth. Our excellent guide, Avishai, began to tell us the sad story of the Dead Sea. Why sad? Because the Dead Sea is receding. The Dead Sea is located in the Syria-Africa Rift Valley, the longest fault line in the world, between Israel and Jordan. Avishai explained that the cataclysmic separation of the Sinai tectonic plate from the Arabian plate resulted in almost identical features on both sides of the valley, although separated by about 60 miles north to south. To illustrate this, he mentioned that the copper ore in Israel's Timna Valley is replicated by similar deposits to the north and east in Jordan.

The Dead Sea is shared equally by Israel and Jordan, who are both responsible for its yearly depletion. The main reason for the large lake's shrinkage – besides meager rainfall - is that since 1960, the Jordan River flow has been diverted, to a large extent, to provide water for drinking after it reaches Lake Kinneret, leaving only a relative trickle to reach its ultimate destination in the Dead Sea. Also significant towards reducing the Jordan's flow are Israel's construction of the Degania dam on the Jordan River, as well as Syria's dam on the Yarmukh River and Jordan's Abdullah Canal. The role that industry plays in the depletion of the sea is relatively small by comparison.

Our hike began with a steep 1.5 mile ascent from Maale Rehaf (Rehaf Heights). Twice, we diverted from the main path to see waterfalls and pools. I can't emphasize enough how beautiful the landscape was from the beginning to the end of our trek. While we were resting at the Rehaf pool, Avishai discussed the subject of what constitutes a "desert". While most of us associate deserts with Lawrence of Arabia, the Arabian Desert is not the most typical kind – although it's the world's largest "hot" desert. Avishai explained that each type of desert has different attributes. The main differentiation is between hot and cold deserts. Compare the immense sand dunes of the Arabian Desert to the world's largest desert, Antarctica, which is all ice.

The Judean Desert, in which we were hiking, has large barren expanses of gravel plains and rocky outcrops. All deserts have one thing in common: there is more evaporation than rainfall. All this was a preamble to the discussion of flash floods. A few years ago, quite close to where we sat, four experienced hikers drowned after a flash flood surprised them. Even more shocking was the fact that two of them were suspended on ropes (rappelling) at the time! The hard-packed, impenetrable ground of the small canyon in which they were hiking allowed the flood water to rise many yards, almost instantly, trapping them. We were suitably warned.

At the next pond that we visited (both ponds were dry or nearly so, as is the usual case in the desert except after a hard rain), Avishai described the wide range of fauna that inhabits the Judean desert, from wild asses to leopards. We learned that camping next to a water source is prohibited because it would inhibit animals from coming to drink at night. In some areas it's forbidden to remain near the water even in the late afternoon, as we learned last year, when a ranger requested us to move on after our late lunch break by a water hole.

Returning to the main trail, we enjoyed a two-mile, almost flat walk along the desert plain, with stunning vistas at every turn. Our final ascent was to Mt. Elazar, where we were treated to a stunning view of Masada (fortress in Hebrew) from an unusual angle. We approached Masada from the southwest, and its grandeur was awesome. We could see remnants of the Roman forts that had surrounded it, the rampart Jewish slaves were forced to build to the summit, and some of the ruins on Masada's summit.

But the story Avishai chose to tell us was of the Zealots who defied the Roman 10th Legion after the fall of Jerusalem in 70 CE. The Zealots had been fighting the Romans for three generations. Their leader was Elazar ben Yair. The story of Elazar and the Zealots comes to us from the writing of Flavius Josephus, the turncoat Jewish general who became the Roman emperor's historian. Josephus describes how, when the Romans had nearly completed the rampart to the top of Masada in the spring of 73 CE, Elazar convinced the 960 warriors and their families to commit mass suicide. They did this rather than be slain or put into slavery by the Romans. Not only did the Romans find the corpses of the Jews when they finally reached Masada's summit, they found plentiful foodstuffs that Elazar had ordered not to be destroyed, the better to show the Romans that the Jews had willingly died, rather than submit.

The history – or legend – of Masada is writ large in the Israeli consciousness. Most Israelis glorify the extremist ethos of the Zealots' suicide, while others criticize it. We all had been to the top of Masada as tourists, or at ceremonies for the induction of our children into the Israel Defense Forces, which are often carried out at monumental sites like Masada. School children learn

Elazar's speech to the Zealots, as reported by Josephus: "…We were the very first that revolted [against Rome], and we are the last that fight against them; and I cannot but esteem it as a favor that God has granted us, that it is still in our power to die bravely, and in a state of freedom ..." These are words that resonate among most Israelis today, still fighting for our independence while surrounded by many who will never accept a Jewish state. (www.parks.org.il/)

The long descent from Mt. Elazar would have been anticlimactic after Avishai's rendition of the Masada story, except that it was the most grueling part of our hike. We slowly made our way down from the 1,200 ft. high summit to the parking lot of the beautiful youth hostel at Masada's base. All the way down from the heights we enjoyed Jordan's colorful Edomite Mountains on the other side of the rift valley, with their changing reddish hues amplified by the setting sun. Often there's a mist in the area which obscures the view, but this time we enjoyed a panorama so clear that everything stood out in precise detail. It was a great ending to a fantastic outing.

HIKING MT. VISHAY AND EN GEDI

"Difficult" was ESRA's description of our latest hike. We had looked forward to this trek both to test ourselves and to explore higher terrain than we usually come across at the Dead Sea. Our expectations were amply fulfilled.

We journeyed by bus past Beersheba through the desert to the familiar En Gedi National Park, where we had hiked before on numerous occasions. The park faces the Dead Sea in Israel's southern region. It is composed of mountainous terrain, several springs and waterfalls, and two wadis. This time we ambitiously set off for the highest point in the park, Mt. Yishay, which is 390 feet (100 meters) *above* sea level. While this may not sound like much, we began the journey close to the shoreline of the Dead Sea, far *below* sea level.

Departing from the En Gedi Field School, the oldest educational institution of its type in Israel, we headed straight up the mountain. Because this part of the hike is in the full glare of the sun, we were happy that it was November. The sunny but cool conditions were ideal, ensuring that we didn't suffer heat exhaustion. Even so, we had been cautioned to bring 3 liters of water per person, which proved to be just about right.

We climbed the steep, stony face of Mt. Yishay for about two hours before reaching the summit. While we had enjoyed beautiful views along the route, these were surpassed by the panorama which awaited us at the top. As we looked out over the Dead Sea, with Jericho to the north, Jordan to the east, and Masada to the south, our excellent guide explained some of the problems which the Dead Sea currently faces.

Sinkholes have been appearing all along the Dead Sea shore in recent years. The En Gedi kibbutz, founded in 1956, has been particularly endangered by the pits during recent decades. The sinkholes are caused by the drop of 30% in the water table which supports the Dead Sea. Large areas of the date palm plantations which the kibbutz cultivates have been abandoned and the motor route along the sea has been diverted in places. So far, there is little that can be done to prevent the occurrence of the pits, which are sometimes large enough to swallow a bus!

Our excellent guide then told us about the Red Sea – Dead Sea conduit plan to divert water from the Red Sea to replenish the Dead Sea, the plan favored by the World Bank. While 1.3 billion cubic meters of water once flowed from the Jordan River into the Dead Sea, the total has currently been reduced to less than one tenth of that. The drop is explained by the water management programs of Israel and Jordan for the Jordan River. For example, a huge amount of the flow is diverted to farmers on both sides of the river to supply them with subsidized water with which to grow crops requiring excessively large amounts of water, such as mangos and bananas.

Our guide opposed the World Bank plan and pointed out that Israel is a world leader in sea water desalination. Israel's increasing number of desalination plants and wastewater recovery efforts will increase our supply of potable and non-potable water, but it's doubtful that the Jordan River's flow to the Dead Sea would be increased, due to Israel's growing population.

After leaving the Mt. Yishay heights we continued back down the mountain and crossed over the Dry Canyon, where we enjoyed shade for the first time that day. We stopped for lunch at a lovely spot with unusual rock ledges alongside the sparsely-filled river bed. We were hurried away from that area by a park ranger, to ensure that the animals who watered there would not be disturbed at their usual afternoon drink. We followed the Zaffit Path eastwards through narrow crevasses to the Dry Waterfall, which afforded us fantastic views of the Dead Sea and the Moabite Mountains in Jordan, after which we emerged from the canyon.

We took another break at the beautiful En Gedi Spring. Our guide explained that the kibbutz was using its allocation of the spring water to distribute En Gedi Mineral Water, a popular brand in Israel. The kibbutz members themselves drink less expensive well water to preserve the valuable spring water as an economic resource. After our respite under the trees by the spring's natural pool, we made a rocky descent past Shulamit's Spring and eventually came to the first of two waterfalls. Along the way we encountered, at a distance, some of the park's wildlife, which included ibex and conies – which wander the region during daylight – as well as vultures, eagles, and falcons.

The last part of our hike was through Wadi David, where the young David, destined to become king of Israel, hid from the jealous King Saul, who had come to slay his ambitious rival. "Behold, David is in the wilderness of En Gedi." {Samuel 1:24:2} There we joined many sightseers at the park's major attraction, David's Waterfall, which is near the entrance. Our hike was completed in late afternoon, after our long and exciting day. Though this trek was more difficult than most ESRA hikes, all of us completed it successfully while thoroughly enjoying one of Israel's most scenic trails.

PERFECT WEEKEND – THE NEGEV AND SDE BOKER

It was the perfect weekend to head south. Michal and I left Alfe Menashe (elevation 1,000 feet) and we were treated to a view unlike any we had previously seen in Israel. It was a clear, sunny day with a huge cloud below us, hovering over the coastal plain. Most striking was the shining tip of the highest skyscaper in greater Tel Aviv peeking above the enormous cloud. But we quickly left all that behind as we and our friends drove south towards Beersheba. We planned to travel to the Negev Desert to several different sites, ranging from prehistoric to ancient to modern.

As we bypassed the modern city of Beersheba, we decided to visit the imposing Negev Brigade Memorial looming above us. The memorial was designed by Dani Karavan, a well-known Israeli sculptor, who is a pioneer of land art. These artistic earthworks incorporate their environmental setting and the passage of time as elements of the sculpture. The monument, finished in 1968, took five years to construct. It honors the Palmach Negev Brigade, which fought bravely in the desert during Israel's War of Independence. From the monument we had a fantastic view of both the desert and the city of Beersheba.

The architecture of Karavan's monument, which is composed of 18 concrete elements, symbolizes the Palmach's indispensable role in the war. The Palmach was Israel's pre-state army, composed of part-time volunteers. On the site there is a perforated tower which alludes to a watchtower shelled with gunfire, the pipeline tunnel, which is reminiscent of the Negev water channel defended by the soldiers, and other shapes and containers which represent significant aspects of the brigade's battles. The concrete walls are engraved with the names of the soldiers who died in the war, the badge of the Palmach, diary passages from the soldiers, the history of the brigade's most important battles, verses, and songs. (www.wikipedia.com)

We left the memorial and continued a few miles south to Tel Sheva, which is the mound on which have been found the archeological remains of ancient Beersheba. "Now he [Isaac] went up from there to Beersheba. And the Lord appeared to him the same night and said, I am the God of Abraham your father. Fear not, for I am with you and will favor you with blessings and multiply your descendants for the sake of My servant Abraham. And Isaac built an altar there and called on the name of the Lord and pitched his tent there; and there Isaac's servants were digging a well. With Isaac, God came first. Before doing anything else in the new place, he built an altar and then waited there to call upon the Lord. Second came his home; he pitched his tent. Third came his business; his servants dug a well." (Genesis 26:23-25)

Built on a low hill on the bank of a dry river bed which flows with water during the winter rainy season, the site has a shallow aquifer ensuring a year-round supply of water. The name Beersheba either comes from seven oaths mentioned in the Bible, or from the seven wells which are found there. Beersheba symbolized the southern boundary of the Land of Israel, as mentioned several times in the Bible: from Dan to Beersheba. The first thing you see upon entering the archeological park is a replica of the "horned" alter which Isaac built to the Lord, using well-dressed stones found on the site. Much of the excavation was done more than 30 years ago, uncovering several layers of settlements, from fortified towns of the early Israelite period to the period of the kings of Judah.

The town was at its zenith from the 10th to the 8th centuries BCE, when it was the southern regional capital of the Kingdom of Judah. King Sennacherib of Assyria destroyed the town during his campaign against Judah in 701 BCE, after which it had no particular significance until modern times. For us, the most amazing part of the excavation was the huge underground water system, complete with giant cisterns, which stored the water needed during the long dry season. (Read more about Tel Sheva at www.israel-mfa.gov.il)

On the way to Sde Boker, our ultimate destination, we stopped for several hours at a modern oasis in the desert, Neve Midbar (Desert) Spa. The spa has four thermal mineral water pools, whose waters originate in natural underground pools and are said to be more than 10,000 years old. We lounged by the very warm outdoor pool and enjoyed the several progressively hotter indoor pools as well.

A few more minutes on the road brought us to Sde Boker, the kibbutz made famous when David Ben-Gurion retired there with his wife Paula. It had always been Ben-Gurion's dream that the Negev would be Israel's crown jewel, a prophecy that has yet to be fulfilled. But hastening that dream is the Midreshet Sde Boker, adjacent to the kibbutz, where we stayed at the Hamburg Field School, a learning center with housing for students and tourists. "Midresha" means a place of learning, which this town in the middle of the desert exemplifies. Ben-Gurion said, "… this is the purpose of Midreshet Sde Boker. We seek to build a scientific research and teaching center which will be a source of moral inspiration and courage, rousing people to a sense of mission, noble, creative and fruitful."

There are dozens of research and educational institutions here, specializing in desert studies, the largest of which is part of the Ben-Gurion University of the Negev, which has its main campus in Beersheba. In addition to college and university studies, there are secondary schools for younger students who want to specialize in environmental and other related studies. We were surprised to see the growing clusters of beautiful desert villas, owned not only by educators and researchers, but by a growing community of pensioners and others who love living in a desert locale. More information can be found on Sde Boker at www.boker.org.il.

The highlight of our weekend was the hike through the adjacent Wilderness of Zin, a fabulous landscape with a strong biblical history: "Then your south quarter shall be from the wilderness of Zin along by the coast of Edom, and your south border shall be the outmost coast of the salt sea eastward: And your border shall turn from the south to the ascent of Akrabbim, and pass on to Zin: and the going forth thereof shall be from the south to Kadesh Barnea …" (Numbers 34:3-4)

We followed Nahal Zin, which is dry except during the infrequent and dangerous flash floods during the rainy season - winter. The rough mountain scenery is composed of outcroppings of flint, used for making tools in ancient times, soft chalk, and non-porous clay which trapped the infrequent rain. The views are as dramatic as one can find in Israel, making the Zin Wilderness a popular site for both trekkers like us and others on jeep tours. As we finished our half-day hike from the heights to the lowest levels of the canyon and back up again, we emerged at the site of the tomb of Ben-Gurion and his American-born wife Paula. Their graves, accessed by a beautiful path which mimicked the course of Nahal Zin, faced one of the most spectacular views of the imposing canyon. It was a sublime end to a great weekend, which included a tasty Italian meal at a restaurant in Beersheba during our 2-hour road trip back to the center of Israel.

ANCIENT HISTORY AT QUMRAN

Israel is famous as a crossroads of the ancient world and is venerated by four religions (Judaism, Christianity, Islam, Baha'i). There are many historical sites and museums which allow visitors to imagine what life may have been like thousands of years ago. Jews have a remarkable memory for their own history. For example, the Passover *haggadah* (arrangement of the service) specifically states that we must recite the history of our exodus from Egypt every year, so that we will all feel like we were present at that historic event which defined the Jews as a people.

Recent archeological finds in Israel have been featured prominently in the media. On a recent visit to the Israel Museum, we saw a 2,200-year-old stone block inscribed in ancient Greek that is concrete evidence of the events leading to the Maccabean Revolt. The artifact is a stele, a carved, commemorative slab, which describes events in Jerusalem in the 2nd century BCE, in the reign of Seleucus IV Philopator. At that time the Jews were part of the Seleucid Empire.

Only three years after the death of Alexander the Great in 323 BCE, his regent was assassinated and the empire was divided. The general Ptolemy became the ruler of Egypt. Eight years later Seleucus I, also a general, took over Babylon and the huge eastern part of Alexander's empire, which extended as far as India. In 198 BCE, Antiochus III became the next great leader of the Seleucid Empire, defeating the Ptolemies and incorporating Egypt into his empire.

The son of Antiochus III, Seleucus IV Philopator, ruled over Greater Syria (which included Palestine), Mesopotamia,

Babylonia and Persia for twelve years, beginning in 187 BCE. To pay the tribute required of him by Rome, Seleucus IV taxed the Jews heavily. The first inscription on the 2,200-year-old stele appoints Heliodorus overseer of Palestine and orders him to seize the treasures of the Temple in Jerusalem. The other two inscriptions, dating from 178 BCE, are shorter notes transmitting the directives of the King from Heliodorus to his subordinates. What is most significant about this archeological find is its validation of the need for the Seleucid rulers to plunder the Jewish Temple.

Antiochus IV, brother of Seleucus IV, found it necessary to conquer Jerusalem because the Jews resisted the occupation of their country by the Hellenists (the Seleucid empire was based on Alexander's Greek background), but his heinous rule resulted in a massive revolt. Antiochus' soldiers slaughtered swine in the Temple and roasted them on the sacred alter. They tried to force the captured Jewish soldiers to eat the forbidden meat. When the Jews refused, Antiochus' soldiers cut out the Jews' tongues, scalped them, cut off their hands and feet and burned them on the alter. In 164 BCE the Jews, led by Judah Maccabee, defeated Antiochus' mighty armies. Antiochus IV died in 164 BC while leading his own army to try to defeat the rebellious Jews.

By 63 BCE the Romans had replaced the Hellenists as the great power in the region. They empowered the Hasmonean king, Hyrcanus II, but he was subservient to the Roman governor of Damascus. The Jews were hostile to the new regime and there were frequent insurrections in the following years. The Hasmonean dynasty ended when Herod, a gentile Idumaean, married the last Hasmonean heir, the Jewish daughter of Hyrcanus

II. From that time, the Land of Israel became a province of the Roman Empire.

Herod the Great became one of the most powerful monarchs in the eastern part of the Roman Empire when he was installed as King of Judea by the Romans in 37 BCE, but he failed to win the trust and support of the Jews. He was granted almost unlimited autonomy in the country's internal affairs, but as a puppet of Rome, he was hated.

Herod was a great admirer of Greco-Roman culture, which he emulated when he built his summer palace. "Herodion" is situated on a high plateau overlooking the Judean Desert, not far from Jerusalem. It is one of the many amazing architectural accomplishments of Herod, which include the Masada fortress, the port of Caesarea, and rebuilding the Second Temple.

Within ten years of Herod's death in 4 BCE, the Romans began direct administration in Judea. A full-scale revolt began in 66 CE, caused by growing anger against increased Roman suppression of Jewish religious life. The superior Roman forces led by General Titus razed Jerusalem in 70 CE and defeated the last Jewish outpost, Masada, three years later. Under the Romans' heavy handed rule, there were scores of sects which banded together for either religious or military motives.

One such sect was the Essenes. The Jewish general turned Roman historian, Flavius Josephus, described the Essenes in his writings. "The Essenes are Jews by race, but are more closely united among themselves by mutual affection, and by their efforts to cultivate a particularly saintly life... They make a point of having their skin dry and of always being clothed in white garments... Before sunrise they recite certain ancestral prayers to the sun as though entreating it to rise. They work until about 11 A.M. when they put on ritual loincloths and bathe for purification. Then they enter a communal hall, where no one else is allowed, and eat only one bowlful of food for each man. They eat in silence ... Afterwards they lay aside their sacred garments and go back to work until the evening ... They see bodily pleasure as sinful ... Those desiring to enter the sect are not allowed immediate entrance. They are made to wait outside for a period of one year. During this time each postulant is given a hatchet, a loincloth and a white garment. The hatchet is used for cleanliness in stooling [defecating] for digging and covering up the hole ... They are not allowed to alter the books of the sect ... They are so scrupulous in matters pertaining to the Sabbath day that they refuse even to go to stool on that day ... They despise danger: they triumph over pain by the heroism of their convictions, and consider death, if it comes with glory, to be better than the preservation of life. They died in great glory amidst terrible torture in the war against the Romans. They believe that their souls are immortal, but that their bodies are corruptible ..."

The Essenes have become well known to us because of an amazing discovery made in 1947 at Qumran, on the northwestern shore of the Dead Sea. A young Arab shepherd was throwing rocks into one of the many caves in the area when he heard something break. While investigating, he found a great many ancient scrolls stored in clay jars and preserved by the arid desert climate. These scrolls, some of which pertained to the Essenes, later proved to be invaluable and were the stuff of an Indiana Jones-type fantasy. Many of them are housed today in the Shrine of the Book in the Israel Museum. The scrolls have proven to be the most ancient Hebrew texts yet recovered, dating back to before the sacking of Jerusalem by the Romans.

We toured the Qumran National Park on a recent trip to the Dead Sea, which is a popular tourist site, fascinating for both Jews and Christians. It has an amazing gift shop, the largest we've seen at any national park. We watched a short but informative film and then toured the archeological park. We saw the remains of the central dining room, a kitchen, a laundry room, ritual baths, and the Scriptorium - a writing room. There were also numerous remains which probably were cattle pens, kilns, pottery workshops, etc.

From the description of Flavius Josephus we known that the Essenes were fanatic about cleanliness, attested to by the large bathing facilities. Also interesting was the fact that their waste was buried away from the dwellings, in a place that has been identified today. It is said that John the Baptist was one of the initiates who spent time at Qumran, but he left without becoming a full member of the sect. This conjecture about John the Baptist stirs Christian interest in the site.

For Christians, the Essenes represent a sect that was contemporaneous with Jesus, which stipulated a way of life that echoed some of his teachings. For Jews, the Essenes are representative of the many sects that proliferated in the Land of Israel in ancient times. Since the scrolls discovered at Qumran were written before the Roman conquest, they give us an invaluable look at what Jewish thought was at the time, pure and simple. Both Jewish and Christian religious scholars still study the scrolls today. Recently, Israeli researchers have perfected a method of piecing together thousands of torn segments of scrolls by matching the DNA of the fragments of hide of which the scrolls are made.

Qumran was populated by Jews as far back as the 8th century BCE. The Essenes lived there from the end of the 2nd century BCE until 68 CE, when the town was conquered by the Romans, just two years before they sacked Jerusalem. A Roman garrison was stationed there in 132-135 CE, during the Bar Kochba revolt. The story of the Essenes is one small entry in the fascinating history of Ancient Israel.

SOUTH TO THE ARAVA AND TIMNA VALLEY

Instead of driving five hours straight on the first day of our mini-vacation, we stopped in the Arava Valley, a desert in the Syria-Africa rift near the Jordanian border and the Red Sea resort of Eilat. We visited Tamar archeological park, where we were quickly drawn towards "Abraham's Tree", which is at least 1,000 years old. (There is a similar tree of the same name in Hebron.) We could easily imagine that this magnificent jujube tree has existed since the days of the patriarchs.

The remains of several fortresses at Ein (a spring) Hatseva are found on this low hill in the Arava Valley, about 20 miles south of the Dead Sea. The strategic position of the hill on the ancient Spice Route impelled the construction of consecutive fortresses over a 1,000 year period, beginning in King Solomon's reign, from about 970 to 928 BCE. "Pharaoh king of Egypt had come up and captured Gezer; he destroyed it by fire, killed the Canaanites who dwelt in the town, and gave it as dowry to his daughter, Solomon's wife. So Solomon fortified Gezer, lower Beth-horon, Baalith, and Tamar in the wilderness, in the land of Judah." (1 Kings 9:16-18) The fortresses all had a dual function, as both a caravansary (caravan station) and a regional military / administrative center. Tamar was the southern boundary of the Land of Israel according to the Bible (Ezekiel 47:13).

By the 8-9th century BCE, the original fortress had become the inner fortress of a much larger garrison with massive defenses, which was a central component of the Kingdom of Judah's border defenses. But its importance declined; by the 7th century BCE, it was taken over by the Edomites, who built a temple within the smaller, rebuilt fortress. During Josiah's religious reforms at the end of the 7th century BCE, the Edomite temple was probably destroyed and the ritual objects broken. During the Roman and Byzantine periods, the fortress was one of many fortifications guarding the border of the Negev Desert, to prevent the penetration of nomadic tribes and to safeguard the profitable trade routes leading to the Mediterranean ports. It is these remains that one can explore today. (www.jewishvirtuallibrary.org)

After touring the Tamar Park, we drove onto the scenic Peace Road hugging the Jordanian border, where we saw the fulfillment of another biblical prophecy. "The desert and the parched land will be glad; the wilderness will rejoice and blossom like the crocus." (Isaiah 35:1) Because of adjustments that were made as part of the peace treaty with Jordan, we were able to drive along the Arava riverbed, which largely marks the border between Israel and Jordan. The "border" is just a chain link fence, with two types of adjacent gravel roads - smooth and rough - for tracking the rare infiltrator. There are several lovely vistas along the Jewish National Fund-built road. Travelers drive by, or can walk through, the amazing giant rock formations known as Badlands near Moshav Idan. We saw a large reservoir, one of 180 that the JNF has built since the late 1980s, which "are an integral part of JNF plans for supplying water over the long term." At least 75 more reservoirs are on the planning board. (www.JNF.org)

After passing palm plantations and a surprising amount of farming in green houses and outdoors under plastic sheeting, we reached our destination for the day, Sapir, which is the county seat for the surrounding moshavim. A small residential and administrative village, Sapir has a beautiful recreation center, including a man-made lake, which was also constructed by the JNF. We stayed over at our friends' small home, provided to them by the local administration at a subsidized rental. The couple are both teaching in the school system and are enjoying desert living with their two small sons. Before sunset we enjoyed a hike in the stark mountains outside of town, climbing a trail which was created when the Syria-Africa rift, which stretches from Syria to Mozambique, was formed.

The following morning we entered the Timna Valley. Timna, one of Israel's grandest outdoor recreation areas, is about 20 miles north of Eilat. Timna resembles a canyon, but unlike most canyons, which have both an entrance and an exit, Timna has just one way in and out. The 27-sq. mile Timna Valley is U-shaped with yellow sandstone mountains, about 1,000 feet high. The red-hued, volcanic Mt. Timna is at the center. The scale of the Timna Valley is huge for Israel, reminding me of a smaller version of a national park in the American West. We drove and walked through some of the amazing rock formations, which have names like the Mushroom and King Solomon's Pillars, and saw examples of age-old wall paintings.

Speaking of King Solomon, the copper mines in the valley are sometimes erroneously labeled "King Solomon's Mines". As we saw in the excellent film at the visitors' center, the mines date back to about 5,000 BCE, when the rich copper ore deposits in the valley attracted miners from ancient Egypt. "Mining activities in the Timna Valley reached a peak during the reign of the Pharaohs of the 14th-12th centuries BCE, when Egyptian mining expeditions, in collaboration with Midianites and local Amalekites, turned the Timna Valley into a large-scale copper industry. A small Egyptian temple dedicated to Hathor, Egyptian goddess of mining, was erected during the reign of Pharaoh Seti I [1318-1304 BCE] and served the members of the Egyptian mining expeditions and their local coworkers. ... In the middle of the 12th century BCE, the mines at Timna and the Hathor temple were abandoned. However, pagan activities in the temple were restored by the Midianites, who remained in Timna for a short period after the Egyptians left. The evidence of a sophisticated Midianite culture, as found in Timna, is of extraordinary importance in the light of the biblical narrative of the meeting of Moses and Jethro, high priest of Midian, and the latter's participation in the organization of the Children of Israel in the desert. (Exodus 18)" (www.mfa.gov.il/MFA/History)

Though some mining in the valley was conducted in the 20th century, today the Timna Valley is strictly an important historical and recreational site, which doubles as a venue for cultural events like the annual dance festival, which had just ended the evening before we arrived. After leaving the park, we drove the short distance to Eilat, where we spent the next several days at the Thai-themed Orchid Hotel. As usual, our pleasant stay in Eilat was highlighted by bathing and snorkeling in the Red Sea, hanging out by the pool, and enjoying the excellent food and tax-free shopping.

Thousands of Israeli-Arabs were on holiday in Eilat, celebrating the Muslim holiday Id-al-Fitr (the Feast of Fast Breaking) at the conclusion of the month of Ramadan. This was a good example of Arabs and Jews intermingling easily, which is not so common. In any event, we plan to visit the Arava Valley again soon, to see some of its many other attractions.

THE ARAVA VALLEY'S PIONEERING AGRICULTURE

Tu Bishvat, the 15th day of the month of Shvat, is our new year of the trees. In 1901, the Jewish National Fund adopted it as a Zionist holiday and it has become customary for a million Israelis and tourists to plant seedlings in celebration of the festival. We decided to spend the holiday in the Arava Valley of the Negev Desert, where an outstanding agricultural fair is held yearly.

We drove south, stopping in Dimona for brunch at the town's new, gleaming mall. Dimona is one of Israel's "development towns", dating back to the vision of David Ben-Gurion in the early years of the state. It was populated mostly with immigrants from the Magreb (Arab North Africa). Today, Dimona is the third largest city in the Negev, with a population close to 40,000, including many immigrants from the former Soviet Union and several thousand members of the Black Hebrews sect, a community originally from Chicago.

After our meal, we continued on to Sapir, the administrative center of the six agricultural villages in the Arava Valley. There we boarded a bus to visit some of the many sites that the Israel Water Utility, Mekorot, constructs and maintains. Mekorot provides 90% of Israel's drinking water and 70% of the total water needs of the country. It has 3,000 installations throughout Israel, providing pure water, desalinized water, sewerage reclamation, rain enhancement, infrastructure, and more. Though Mekorot is owned by the government, it and Israel Electric Corporation are at the top of the list of companies still to be privatized. Mekorot is part of the knowledge base that makes Israel a leader in the export of water technology around the world.

217

Underneath the Arava Valley is a vast lake of water, which Mekorot has developed at its three regional centers. The result is the huge agricultural growth of the area. We were particularly impressed by the large reservoir which we visited, which has a gigantic plastic bladder in which the water rests. This bladder protects the water from debris after the rare desert flash floods, and from evaporation. Equally impressive is the process by which the company filters the water from the underground lake to create five quality levels, from water for drinking to water for agricultural use. At our friends' house in Sapir we were shown the three separate water systems that all the desert homes utilize: one for drinking, one for washing, and one for all other use.

A fascinating detail we learned about Israel's water technology is the fact that after the Six Day War of 1967, Mekorot began developing water resources beyond the Green Line, the 1949 Armistice Line. Consequently, when a peace treaty was signed in 1994 with Jordan, land was traded between the two countries to allow Israel to maintain the water infrastructure. Other land was leased by Israel from Jordan for the same purpose. In both cases, Jordan benefits from Israel's water technology and its agricultural expertise.

That evening we had a treat. Although we weren't specifically invited, we joined hundreds of others for an evening of free entertainment at the fairground. There was a large (unheated) tent with scores of tables and numerous bars and buffets with snacks, hot cider, beer, wine, soft drinks. Eventually, we succumbed to the cool temperature and headed to our guest house for a good night's sleep.

The next morning we boarded another bus, this one to view three of the many farms in the region. The Arava Valley is home to about 450 active farms, which produce half of the fresh agricultural exports from Israel and a great part of the produce for domestic consumption. Our first stop was a pepper farm. The farmer, who had previously grown flowers, explained how it was necessary to stay several steps ahead of the international competition to sustain high profits. When countries such as India and Ethiopia (where some Israeli farmers have relocated) began selling flowers at the international market in Brussels - which operates like a commodity exchange - many flower growers in Israel found new crops to specialize in. These include hot-house tomatoes, and, in this case, peppers. Utilizing the latest agricultural expertise, the peppers were planted in shallow tubs irrigated by the drip method, an Israeli innovation.

The most amazing thing about the process is that only 30% of the drip water is absorbed, allowing the balance to be saved and used for several other crops. The last of the remaining water ended up going to the date palm plantation owned by the farmer's son. Our guide told us that the Arava farms were so profitable that a farmer had only to dream about selling his farm and he would find a bunch of would-be buyers at his door in the morning.

We next visited an organic farm, the first of its kind in the Arava, whose crops are mostly bought by a large American importer, and a flower farm, whose owner was clever enough to still make money selling his crop at the Brussels flower market. On the three farms we noticed the laborers, who are from South and Southeast Asia, but primarily Thailand. We then returned to the exhibition grounds to explore the many exhibits. We'd never seen so many varieties of vegetables in our lives, not to mention the flowers. There were all kinds of companies showing their wares, from seeds, to equipment, to buildings, and much more. We enjoyed both the exhibits and the abundant free food, as well as the displays of Southeast Asian folk dancing. We learned that the Center for Agricultural Training brings some of these young workers to Israel to learn many technical subjects pertaining to agriculture. They take this knowledge home when they leave Israel - with a small fortune in savings to start a new life in their homeland.

Afterwards, we drove a short distance to hike in one of the Negev's most challenging sites, Ein Tamar, a dry waterfall which plunges downward to the Dead Sea plain. We descended several long ladders set in the cliff face (one was 60 feet high!) and scrabbled down rocks via a swinging rope. The gorgeous view of the desert as we left the narrow crevasse was a stupendous reward for our efforts.

The next morning we took a scenic route through two of Israel's incredible machteshim and ascended to higher ground via the spectacular Aqrabbim (or Scorpion) Ascent, mentioned in the Bible in both Numbers and Joshua. The tortuous route was used by the Romans for access from the central Negev towards the Red Sea and by Israeli troops in 1948, on their way to Eilat. Until the present road to Eilat was built, this serpentine road was the main route from the north. We continued on towards home, enjoying the tail end of our Tu Bishvat vacation in Israel's scenic and productive desert region.

TEL TZAVIT AND THE PHILISTINES

We started our midweek ESRA hike early and soon reached our starting point near Kibbutz Kfar Menachem, which is located southwest of Jerusalem, between Ashdod and Bet Shemesh. It was a perfect February day; a light jacket or fleece sufficed until midday, when most of us stowed our top layers in our daypacks due to the hot sun. The kibbutz was founded in 1935 as a moshav and named after Menashe Osishkin, a pioneer from Russia who worked diligently for the revival of the Hebrew language and Jewish settlement, in what was then part of the Ottoman Empire.

Forced to flee in the Arab Revolt of 1936, the moshav's founders rebuilt the settlement as part of the Tower and Stockade program: 57 prefabricated forts assembled overnight in the years 1936-1939, on high ground and in close proximity, to quickly establish Jewish settlement on the land. In 1939, a new group of pioneers, which included a nucleus of young Americans, successfully established the kibbutz. It was relocated to a nearby hill and was expanded after Israel's War of Independence.

We quickly walked to the Haruvit (Carob) Forest, a large and popular park built by the Jewish National Fund. Among the parks 2,000 acres there are conifers, cypresses, Jerusalem pines and wide stretches of broad-leafed trees, such as the eucalyptus and the carob. Fruit trees grow alongside abandoned agricultural terraces and there are wild flowers in abundance. Had this been the weekend, the dirt road we were hiking on would have been full of cars, because the park has many family attractions for short walks and picnicking. In addition, there is a 75-acre "Warrior's

Park" in the heart of the forest, built especially to accommodate the physically challenged.

From afar, we soon saw one of the highlights of the hike, a verdant hill that eventually loomed over us. It was Tel Tzavit, site of the remains of Gath, largest of the five Philistine city-states. Who were the Philistines? They formed part of the great naval confederacy, the "Sea Peoples", who had wandered during the 12th century BCE from their homeland in southern Greece and the Aegean Islands to Canaan, on the eastern shore of the Mediterranean. One hypothesis for this mass exodus is that a great earthquake destroyed the civilizations of Crete and Santorini.

The invading Philistines fought the Egyptians, the ruling power in the area, and were eventually repulsed by Rameses III. However, it is theorized that he was unable to dislodge them from their settlements in Canaan, where they built their city-states: Ashdod, Ashkelon, and Gaza on the seacoast, and Ekron and Gath inland.

Canaan is the name of the land into which the Hebrew tribes finally arrived after the Exodus. Its inhabitants were an assortment of indigenous peoples and others who had wandered into the area. "Canaan was the father of Sidon his firstborn, and of the Hittites, Jebusites, Amorites, Girgashites, Hivites, Arkites, Sinites, Arvadites, Zemarites and Hamathites. Later the Canaanite clans scattered and the borders of Canaan reached from Sidon toward Gerar as far as Gaza, and then toward Sodom, Gomorrah, Admah and Zeboiim, as far as Lasha." (Genesis 10:15-19)

Around the same time, Joshua led the Israelites into Canaan, which for them was the Promised Land, flowing with milk and honey. Centuries later, the army of Israel's first king, Saul, faced the Philistines in the Elah Valley by Tel Tzavit, between the mountain strongholds of the opposing sides. Goliath, the Philistine giant, was slain and beheaded by the shepherd boy, David, and the Philistines fled the battleground. Soon after, Saul and his sons were killed by the Philistines and their bodies hung on the walls of Bet Shean. David became King Saul's successor and Israel's greatest monarch. "How have the mighty fallen, And the weapons of war perished!" (2 Samuel 1:27)

"The Philistine soldiers were tall and clean-shaven. They wore breastplates and short kilts, and rode in chariots drawn by two horses. They carried small shields and fought with straight swords and spears. By contrast, the Israelites had no chariots, horses, or iron weapons. No wonder they quaked at the more advanced, highly educated forces of the Philistines."

"Champion-to-Champion (one-on-one) combat was unknown in Canaan at the time of Goliath's challenge to Saul's Armor. However, Greek (Aegean) mythology was filled with combat between champions/heroes. Thus, Goliath, a descendent of Aegean parents, and having grown up listening to the many Mycenaean myths, probably pictured himself as a Greek deity or champion - like Atlas, or Odysseus, or Hercules of later myth." (www.touryoav.org.il)

Since 1996, excavations at the site have revealed fascinating and unprecedented finds, including the earliest known siege system in the world, the earliest deciphered Philistine inscription, and extremely rich and well-preserved evidence of various cultures, peoples, and historical events, spanning some six millennia of occupation. (www.dig-gath.org) Excavations at the site will eventually include finds from these civilizations: Canaanite/ Philistine (Late Bronze); Israelite (Iron Age); Persian; Roman; Crusader; and Muslim.

"Three of the five Philistine cities – Ashdod , Ashkelon and Gaza – were never entirely lost, because their names have remained almost unchanged until this day. The fourth, Ekron, has been located at Tel Miqneh (at nearby Kibbutz Revadim) and has yielded rich Philistine finds. Mighty Gath eluded scholars the longest. Its ancient name did not survive – it became known in Arabic as Tell es-Safi – "the pure mound" apparently because of its gleaming white chalk cliffs, an element the Crusaders also noticed when they called the fortress they built here Blanche Guarde (the white fortress), remains of which can still be seen." For more about Tel Tzavit, see www.tourism.gov.il.

After descending from the tell, which is about 800 ft. above sea level, we continued through the countryside to the Luzit caves, located at Moshav Luzit. These were very large and beautiful bell-shaped caves. Reuven, our excellent guide, explained how they were built into the soft, white limestone. The builders (most of the caves were built by Arabs during a relatively late period) would dig a hole in the chalky rock and lower themselves into it. From there, they would continue digging and enlarging the opening into what would become a large bell-shaped cave. Some of the caves retain the small opening at the top, while in others the ground has caved in and the opening is large. Wandering around the various caves, many of which open on to each other, was the perfect ending to our enjoyable 8-mile hike.

Note: Where the name "Palestine" came from:

"The name Palestine refers to a region of the eastern Mediterranean coast from the sea to the Jordan Valley and from the southern Negev desert to the Galilee lake region in the north. The word itself derives from 'Plesheth', a name that appears frequently in the Bible and has come into English as 'Philistine'. Plesheth was a general term meaning rolling or migratory. This referred to the Philistine's invasion and conquest of the coast from the sea. The Philistines were not Arabs nor even Semites, they were most closely related to the Greeks originating from Asia Minor and Greek localities. They did not speak Arabic. They had no connection, ethnic, linguistic or historical with Arabia or Arabs.

From the fifth century BCE, following the historian Herodotus, Greeks called the eastern coast of the Mediterranean 'the Philistine Syria' using the Greek language form of the name. In CE 135, after putting down the Bar Kochba revolt, the second major Jewish revolt against Rome, the Emperor Hadrian wanted to blot out the name of the Roman 'Provincia Judaea' and so renamed it 'Provincia Syria Palaestina', the Latin version of the Greek name and the first use of the name as an administrative unit. The name 'Provincia Syria Palaestina' was later shortened to Palaestina, from which the modern, anglicized 'Palestine' is derived. The name Palestine was revived after the fall of the Ottoman Empire in World War I and applied to the territory in this region that was placed under the British Mandate for Palestine." (www.palestinefacts.org)

WADI DARGA AND EIN TAMAR

We began our trip – first to the Arava Valley in the Negev and then to Eilat – at the end of November, a wonderful time for traveling in Israel. We three couples, the usual crew, piled into Jeremy's van and soon had bypassed Beersheba to reach our first stop, Wadi Darga. Part of the Hae'teqim Cliff Nature Reserve, Wadi Darga is a canyon with especially beautiful scenery and many trails. We chose a 3-4 hour route, since we still had far to go to reach our destination before dark.

Hooded crows riding thermal currents accompanied us on parts of our journey which began in the upper part of the canyon. We were struck by the beautifully colored rock walls and the many caves in the cliffs above our heads. Numerous air force jets thundered high in the sky, their roar magnified by echoes off the steep walls, enhancing the grandeur of the canyon.

Wadi Darga is known for its unusual caves with rectangular-shaped entrances. We climbed into the most prominent "Muraba'at Cave", in which explorers in the 1950s found letters written and signed by Bar Kochba, leader of the Second Revolt against Rome in the 2nd century CE. This great warrior, whose legendary status has been validated by the letters, was considered to be a Messiah by the Jewish sage, Rabbi Akiba. The rabbi regarded the commander, Simon Bar Kochba, as a heroic figure who would be able to restore Israel's sovereignty. Rabbi Akiba's belief in Bar Kokhba was based on the Star Prophecy, a verse from Numbers 24:17: "There shall come a star out of Jacob." Bar Kochba means "son of a star" in the Aramaic language.

There were only a few other hikers besides us until we came to the lower part of the canyon, where ropes are necessary to negotiate two steep sections. We found it relatively easy to ascend the first rock wall, in contrast to a group of older hikers who were descending the same narrow opening. After they graciously allowed us to climb past them, we soon found ourselves intermingled with scores of Scouts who were tackling the next difficult, but more open, pitch. The pensioners and the scores of youngsters with their leaders and guards are typical of the many organized trekkers who explore Israel's many scenic trails.

Continuing on, we eventually returned to our van and descended to the Dead Sea road. We arrived shortly at moshav Ein Tamar, where our friends' daughter and her young family live. Ein Tamar (Date Palm Spring) is one of many prospering Arava Valley farming communities. Founded in 1982, Ein Tamar's farmers cultivate winter crops and run tropical fruit and date plantations, assisted by agricultural workers from Thailand. We sampled some of the delicious squash and peppers grown there, when a large carton of produce (not quite good enough for export) was dropped off at our door, as is the custom among the farmers there. We were intrigued to learn that the red and yellow peppers we enjoyed were originally green. We learned that if green peppers are allowed to ripen, they eventually become various colors, according to length of time on the vine.

The moshav, which has shaded, spacious homes, smaller starter homes, and excellent community facilities and infrastructure, impressed us. If all goes as planned, our young friends will eventually have a farm. They plan to grow date palms, for which the area is renowned. If not, the agricultural land is valuable and can be rented to an agriculturist. Desert living is becoming increasingly attractive to young Israelis for both economic and ideological reasons. Compared to the crowded center of Israel, both the North and southern desert regions have much lower living expenses.

After a day spent relaxing at the Bauman home and hiking around the many desert trails nearby, we left Ein Tamar the next morning for our ultimate destination, Eilat. We were to stay at the Rimonim (pomegranates) Hotel, part of the Israeli Rimonim chain. Our friend Ros, a journalist, had booked all of our rooms through the Eilat Journalists Conference, which was convening in Eilat at the time.

We did what we always enjoy doing in Eilat: a day on the Red Sea beach with a long swim in the sea, another day hanging around the pool, shopping at the busy mall in town (Eilat is exempted from Israel's VAT), walking the waterfront promenades, and enjoying the musical entertainment in the hotels. A highlight of our stay was the viewing of the timely and spectacular conjunction of Venus, Jupiter, and the moon. They formed a triangle which changed shape from hour to hour in the evening, and from day to day. In addition, we attended some stimulating events at the journalism conference.

Our trip had many components: hiking, visiting friends at an agricultural village, vacationing, and mingling with journalists. It's just another example of the many great and interesting adventures one can enjoy in Israel.

SHIVTA AND KADESH BARNEA

We traveled to the Kadesh Barnea area in the Negev Desert recently with our usual crew. "And when the Lord sent you from Kadesh Barnea, saying, 'Go up and take possession of the land that I have given you,' then you rebelled against the commandment of the Lord your God and did not believe him or obey his voice." [Deuteronomy 9:23] But more about that later.

After stopping for coffee, homemade bread, and goat cheese at the Cornmehl Farm in the northern Negev, we arrived at Shivta National Park, an ancient Nabatean city. Because of Shivta's size and excellent state of preservation, it's one of the most impressive archeological sites in Israel. The Nabateans were Arab tribes who migrated to the area of southern Jordan and the Negev around 300 BCE, lived in that area for about 1,000 years, and prospered primarily from agriculture and commerce. The Nabateans, who converted to Christianity in the 4th century, built large churches in their cities. At Shivta, we saw ruins of three churches, irrigation channels, a reservoir, and various dwellings and storehouses. The Nabateans appear to have assimilated among the other peoples of the area after the 10th century CE, leaving their habitations intact for newcomers.

The Nabateans were great practitioners of desert agriculture, using advanced irrigation techniques to grow olives, grapes, and other necessities. "Simultaneously, they were maintaining commerce as an income, attending trading routes [such as the Spice Route] that were stretched from the Arabian Peninsula to the Mediterranean Basin along which they were leading caravans loaded with medicinal herbs and incenses. For supplying the needs of these commercial caravans, they had established a net of lodgings-guarded posts [caravansaries], which were placed in a distance of a one day walk from each other. In addition, the Nabateans built big cities." Petra, a UNESCO World Heritage site in Jordan, is their most magnificent monument. (www.tiuli.com)

After touring the sun-bleached city, we had a lovely lunch at the Shivta Farm, right next to the site's parking lot. Clearly a venue for tour groups as well as individuals, the restaurant featured huge tables and freshly made specialties. We admired the farm's beds of herbs: rosemary, thyme, lemon grass and za'atar (wild hyssop), all of which were used liberally in the excellent cuisine served in small, traditional Middle Eastern clay ovens. There are several basic rooms available for overnight guests. The young owners, Ayala and Ami Och, renovated the building, which was erected in the 1930s by H. Colt, the son of the American arms manufacturer, to house groups of archaeologists. We saw Colt's name written in a Greek inscription over the main entrance.

A most interesting story about Shivta dates back to the 1948 War of Independence. The Egyptian army had come from Sinai and controlled most of the Negev, threatening to attack northward to Tel Aviv. General Yigal Allon, commander of the Southern front army based around Shivta, devised a stunning plan to surprise the unsuspecting Egyptians. Utilizing long-forgotten Nabatean trade routes through the desert, Allon's forces surrounded and captured the Egyptian army. Thus archeology came to the aid of modern Israel.

We were heading to the small, dusty village of Azuz, in the Kadesh Barnea region. On the way we visited "Shofars", where the proprietor, Boaz, works with his wife making strictly kosher shofars. Boaz explained to us that the shofar is the oldest musical instrument that we know of, mentioned numerous times in the Bible, most famously in Joshua 6:4-5: "And seven priests shall bear before the ark seven trumpets of rams' horns [shofars]: and the seventh day ye shall compass the city seven times, and the priests shall blow with the trumpets. And it shall come to pass, that when they make a long blast with the ram's horn, and when ye hear the sound of the trumpet, all the people shall shout with a great shout; and the wall of the city shall fall down flat, and the people shall ascend up every man straight before him." We were fascinated to learn from Boaz that during Israeli wars, many religious soldiers have blown shofars while praying.

Boaz told us that a shofar must be made from a kosher horned animal, but not from a cow or bull, a prohibition that dates back to the infamous Golden Calf. Some of the raw horns used are from antelope, oryx, ibex, and sheep; it takes about ten hours of hand-labor to make each shofar. Because of the limited supply, Boaz's shofars aren't found in tourist outlets or Jerusalem's Old City, but must be special-ordered. As Boaz, originally from South Africa, says, "In our shop we hand pick every horn and choose it for its tonal quality and appearance. All our instruments meet the highest standards possible." (www.shofars.com)

Late that afternoon we arrived at Azuz, a small settlement practically on the border with Egypt. Consisting of a handful of families, Azuz is a dusty, hard-scrabble location, but it's not without its surprises. We had booked "rooms" with Eyal and Avigail Hirshfeld and their six delightful young children. Eyal has built the guest lodgings from old buses - "Zimmerbuses". Our hand-detailed lodgings were beautifully redone and certainly comfortable and unique. Avigail, originally from South Africa, prepared lovely meals during our two-day stay, which we ate outdoors.

During the day Eyal took us on a fascinating jeep tour of the Kadesh Barnea area. After a long and bumpy ride through the desert, we came to an area distinctive for its numerous archeological ruins. These were the foundations of small stone huts dating back to 1,400 BCE, in which the Israelites sojourned for at least 19 of their 40 years in the desert! Eyal explained to us: "In this area of Kadesh Barnea, there is clear evidence of the passage of the children of Israel, in exactly the timing of the biblical record! ... This means that the biblical record is perfectly true and exact according to archeological evidence, contradicting the mainstream teaching of most guides in Israel." Eyal based his conclusion on the writings of the iconoclast Dr. Immanuel Velikovsky and especially Yehoshua Etsion's book "The Lost Bible".

Eyal told us that in the Kadesh Barnea area there are many ruins similar to those where we sat, but that this was the only area that had been excavated. He attributed the lack of additional exploration, in part, to the discomfort of mainstream archeologists to deal with this potential discovery: a great mass of people appeared suddenly on the map in these arid areas - out of nowhere - quickly disappeared and then reappeared in Jericho and the rest of Israel. Such a finding would contradict the archeological establishment's timeline, which is based on Egyptologists' findings and theories, not the Bible. In any event, this and many other fascinating sites in the area are very neglected by the Israeli

Antiquities Authority, which attributes incorrect dates to these sites and therefore disregards their true significance, according to Eyal.

Eyal explained that here, as in many other places that have not yet been excavated in the Negev, there are many temporary camping sites, with temporary graves (tumulis) located nearby. Research was done on fragments remaining in these empty graves, and it was determined by an American archeologist who also dug in Jericho, that the people who passed through the Kadesh Barnea area were buried here only temporarily. Their permanent graves were found to the north of Jericho, along the Israelites' exact route of entry into the Land of Israel. (See Eyal's fascinating website: www.exodia.co.il)

On Friday evening at Shabbat dinner, we Hirshfeld guests were joined by others from a nearby zimmer, making a total of a dozen adults and ten children. We enjoyed fresh homemade salads, challah, and a South African-style stew (potjiekos), cooked over a fire pit in a huge iron pot. Due to the cold night air we bundled up in our jackets around the table, but we enjoyed ourselves nonetheless. The long day ended with a game of Yatzee in the sitting area of the bigger of our two Zimmerbuses.

The next day we walked a short distance to a somewhat neglected nature preserve. In sight of a water station of the disused Turkish railroad that once crossed Palestine, this unique oasis in the western Negev highlands has two ancient wells. Its name, Be'erotayim, means "two wells", in this case the wells of the patriarchs Moses and his brother Aaron. The wells and a small forest of tamarisks are sited on an aquifer dating back to the time when prehistoric man lived there. Nearby we found the crossroads for two caravan routes of traders who began crossing the Negev from the end of the second millennium BCE. One was from the Nile delta along the Sinai Peninsula, apparently "The Shur trail" mentioned in Genesis. The other route came from Eilat. At Be'erotayim the routes diverged towards Gaza in the west, and Be'er Sheva and Jerusalem in the northeast.

Our adventure in the southern desert only lasted for a few days, but nevertheless we had a great time exploring Israel's ancient history and enjoying its modern hospitality. After Shivta, the shofar factory, the Hirshfelds' Zimmerbuses, Be'erotayim, and a visit to a local honey producer (we bought a lot), we drove north through Beersheba, checking out the new cultural center in Israel's desert city on our way home.